ARTISTIC MOMENTS

THE INTERNATIONAL LIBRARY OF PHOTOGRAPHY

PICTURE.COM

Gregg Wisniewski, Editor

Artistic Moments

Library of Congress
Cataloging in Publication Data

ISBN 0-7951-5272-8

Printed in China

Published by
The International Library of Photography
3600 Crondall Lane
Suite 101
Owings Mills, MD 21117

FOREWORD

Writing about photography is a difficult task, as it entails the translation of one art form into another. While every photograph may not inspire a thousand words, it is easy to see how the saying evolved. Words are a function of the intellect. But, much like music, a visual image speaks directly to the emotions, evoking an immediate and powerful response. Only when one attempts to analyze, interpret, and critique this image do words come into play.

As one views a photograph, one is slowly taken on a visual journey through the eye of the photographer. Whether the photograph was staged or the "point-and-click method" was employed, the picture represents the fact that moments in time pass within the blink of an eye. The photographer not only captures a scene or a subject; he also creates a lasting, tangible image of a fleeting instant. The beauty of photography is that any individual can produce an image of these passing moments.

Photography represents both an active and a passive art form. The degree to which a photographer participates in his art form varies from photograph to photograph. The photographer can either tell a story within the photograph, or simply stand aside and record life as it happens. The one thing that holds true for all photography is this: without the photographer there can be no photograph. Even in a simple snapshot, the photographer's influence is clearly evident.

The photographs within this anthology exhibit their own importance as well as demonstrate the importance of the photographer. In some cases, the idea or photo found the photographer. For instance, while taking pictures on a nature hike, a photographer may catch the sunset as it breaks through a bunch of trees, and thus an idea may be born. In other instances, a photographer may orchestrate and choreograph the set-up of a photograph in order to fulfill a creative idea or notion. (This may be the case in still-life or abstract photography.)

Another similar element in most of these photographs is the photographer's love of and dedication to his subject. For example, nature photography is often captured by devoted nature watchers. Those people who take humorous photographs usually enjoy the lighter side of life and tend to look for the funniest aspect of any situation. The numerous photographs of children in this book were most likely taken by parents or grandparents who appreciate the joy and wonderment contained in a child's smile. Becoming emotionally involved with a subject, through deep love or interest, often enables a photographer to generate ideas that help him capture the true essence of his subject.

There are also photographers who gain inspiration not from relating to one specific subject or another, but rather from focusing on the photographic process itself. They often use special techniques to create images they have envisioned within their own minds, or they choose to concentrate on one particular aspect of photography (such as lighting) and through experimentation examine its effect on a particular subject. By casting aside conventional approaches, these photographers open different pathways to new ideas, allowing their own imaginations to roam freely.

No matter how or why a photograph is taken, the viewer must realize that each photograph represents an individual's artistic viewpoint. There are many excellent photographs contained in this anthology. At a quick glance they might appear to be just pictures, but be sure to focus on the ideas being conveyed, both emotionally and physically. Allow yourself to become lost in the photo: perhaps you may gain a new understanding of it, or you may simply be able to relate more deeply to the photographer's viewpoint.

Andy Warhol once predicted that in the future everyone will have his fifteen minutes in the spotlight. This philosophy could easily be applied to photography by simply stating that every subject has its moment, and as a photographer, one must strive to find and capture these instants. After all, these cherished moments, which may seem frozen in time when we see them through the camera's viewfinder, do not last fifteen minutes; rather, viewing a photograph that captures these instances may trigger memories that will always remain embedded deep within our minds. Through photographs we are therefore offered a physical reminder as an accompaniment to a memory. We then hold in our hands the permanency of a cherished moment in time—an image of yesterday.

Russell Hall
Senior Editor

Taylor Bencal   Children
I Love You This Much

Tammy A. Fehl   Children
Who Could Say No To Me?

Jennifer Huling   Children
Can You See Me Now?

Forest V. Collins   Nature
The Young And Beautiful; Natural Alaskan Wilderness

Lupe Garcia   Travel
El Majahual Beach, El Salvador, Central America

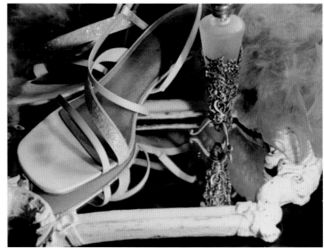

Erica Lee Turchin   Other
To Be A Woman

Barbara J. Leat
Animals/Pets
Cover Girl

Ronald J. Smith
Animals/Pets
Life Is Good

Amanda Weaver
Children
Baby's Big Truck

Phylicia Elisabeth Christianson
Other
Bannister

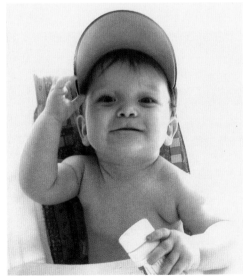

Linda Marie Ellison
Portraiture
Baby

Kim L. Clark
Animals/Pets
Ginger

Beverly Dargento　　　　　　　　　People
Helping Little Hands

Julia Ann Nelson　　　　　　　　　Animals/Pets
Shadow

Elena Gonzalez　　　　　　　　　Nature
Hope At Rest

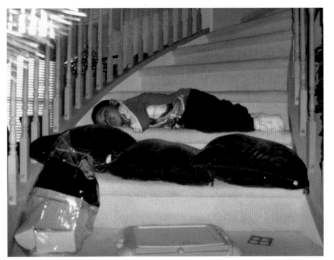

Phelt M. Saucier　　　　　　　　　Children
Timothy Carlton Fleming Bailey; Worn Out On Christmas Day

David A. Rowland　　　　　　　　　Animals/Pets
Bird's Eye View

Josee Carole Duchesneau　　　　　　　People
Flower

Michael R. Atwood Nature
Hurricane Charlie

Renee Michelle Clarke Animals/Pets
Spooky In A Blanket

Migdalia Nieves People
True Love

Kristin Ibsen Animals/Pets
AK, My Beautiful Boy

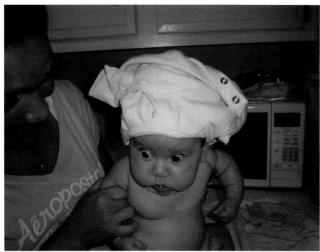

George Ackerbloom Children
Having A Bad Hair Day

Antony Stockford Children
The Bull Wins Again

Miranda Sue Kamphaus Nature
Evening Mist

Karen DeChristopher Animals/Pets
Pepper Plays Fetch

David Alan Cordeiro Children
Children Of War

Natalie M. Paterson Nature
Lightning

Ray Allen Hollis Portraiture
End Of A Day At The Zoo

Kelly Anne Larson Nature
Silence

Casey Sanders Animals/Pets
In The Eyes Of A Neighborhood Cat

Heather Holmes Children
Little Boy Blue

Bill Deane Other
Patriotism Versus Devastation

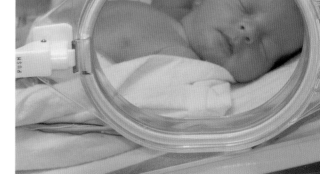

Fred Martin Children
The First Round

Jaclyn Nicole LaMothe Other
Waiting In Line

James P. Goloversic Nature
Back Home

M. Z. Zayan   Nature
Tenacity

Moshe David   Children
Beauty And The Beast

Jennifer Hatten McDougal   Children
On The River Bank

Kelley Bradford   Nature
Ucayali Sunrise

Broni Hazel Paice   Children
Children Of The Night

Wally Johnson   Other
Fall On The Nebo

Bill Amerena   Animals/Pets
My Pal

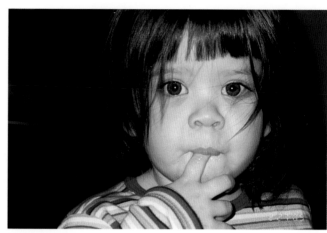

Rachael Talamantes   Children
The Face Of An Angel

Daniel T. Kirkendall   Children
Goldilocks And The Polar Bear

Cathrine Rowland   Nature
Early Morning Snow

Alice Huber   People
Number One Son

Brandy Howard   Portraiture
Wisdom

Julie Vivirito Travel
Art In Jackson Square, New Orleans, Louisiana

Lauren R. Majcher People
The Happy Ballerina

Rebecca Tison People
Son Of Sunrise

Raymond St. Jacques Humor
That's Our Style

Amber LaMar Travel
Eiffel Tower

Brandee Paisano Children
Innocence

Carolynn M. Leeuw   Nature
October Monarch On A Pansy

Karly Roberts   Children
Concentration

Marlene Rose Ruppa   Children
Santa's Sweet Smiles

Rosemary Sisto   Nature
Snow And Ice

James Ware   People
Glass Blower And His Art

LaTonya Scott   People
Untitled

Rose V. Becker   Travel
Untitled

Hannah Elizabeth Bochert   Nature
God's Masterpiece, His Sunset

Lonnie D. Haynes   Nature
Blue Ridge View

Robert McArthur   Nature
Untitled

Susan Danker   People
Ties That Bind

Elizabeth Olguin   Children
Big Brother's First Day At School

Alois Poll Other
Tiere Der Tod Eines Schmetterlings!

Alice Deal Richardson Animals/Pets
Please, Just One More Peanut

Joye J. Dunlop People
Please Pass The Alka-Seltzer!

Angelita Rodriguez Animals/Pets
Spike And Buddha

Joan Kremer Nature
Paradise

Wendy Brantley Children
Peek-A-Boo

Ann Hillsgrove   Nature
Once-In-A-Lifetime Masterpiece Of Nature

Siddharth Mahajan   Other
Sparkling Outburst

Lori Peachey   Children
Want To Go For A Ride?

Loraine Paul   Children
Washing His Clothes Out

Laura J. Ray   Nature
Fall Reflections

Robert D. Price   Humor
And Maybe The Camera Flash Is Too Close

Jennifer Setters   Nature
Water Beauty

Rita Lucier   Other
Scenery

Brittany Simons   Nature
Look Out

Trudy Patterson Colflesh   Nature
Ancient Ponderosa Pine On A Mountain

Laura Boswell   Other
Retired

Marianne King   Animals/Pets
Cat Eyes

Stephanie Chaney
If I Were A Butterfly

Nature

Brice Laub
Untitled

Animals/Pets

Donald Jones
Santa On Bicycle

People

Adam Grandt
Three Inches Of Hail

Nature

Jean Ellsworth
Untitled

Animals/Pets

Tami Lynn McNabb
Farm Buddies

Children

Jennifer L. Miles   Nature
Ah, Nectar, Sweet Nectar!

Dixie Fae Bollin   Animals/Pets
What, Mom?

Rohit Mathur   Animals/Pets
Monstro

LaVerne H. Miller   Animals/Pets
Three Baby Raccoons In Our Backyard

Frederick Simmons   Action
Dead End

Nicole Bradford   Nature
Sunset At Key West Pier

Chris Andrews   Other
On My Way Home

Amanda Madden   People
Return From War

Yazmin Labrador   Animals/Pets
Loli's Rose

Rachel Goodrich   Children
I'm So Pretty

Andrew Opperman   Action
Above The Crowd — The Vans Cup At Tahoe

Christy Renei Turner   Animals/Pets
Sand Crab

Liz Estella Meza   Children
Mama's Boy

Stephen Paul Jennings   Animals/Pets
Chillin' Octopus

William Michael Dooley   Nature
Serenity

Shawn R. Sullins   Other
On The Edge

Danielle Martinez   Animals/Pets
Sunset Beauty

Daniel Edward Klein   Nature
Sunrise At Orient Point, New York

Andy Down Action
Any Grey Poupon?

Nicole Ann Thomas Children
Hunter

George Parascandola Nature
Sunset At Cabezon

Shirley Ann Bogenrief Nature
Sunset Clouds

Dillon Martin Griffin Children
Quieter Than The Gerber Baby

Michelle Dawn Seltzer Children
Playing Chicken

Rachael Marie Pearce   Children
Carli-Belle

Danielle Marie Minney   Children
Vacation Boy

Masaki Arthur Pierce   Travel
Bullet

Claire M. Nice   Travel
Sydney Harbor From Cruise Ship

Scott Barnhill   Nature
Conch

Robert Kalop McKinney   Animals/Pets
One Playful Kitten

Helena W. Guest Animals/Pets
Leopard Hissing

Jen Turner Children
My Girls

Brent Allen Markowski Nature
Forgotten

Niki Sadeghi Other
The First Sunset Of Spring In Vancouver

Laura Lee Lotto Animals/Pets
The Pack

Erin E. O'Brien Travel
Calm Seas

Jenny Sue Harris   Animals/Pets
I Can Tiptoe

Tom Kline   Animals/Pets
Self-Portrait

Regina Lee Champion   Nature
Black And Blue Butterfly

Mike Daugherty   Nature
Point Lobos

Sean Thomas Floegel   Other
Unwinding

John Richard Ryan   Animals/Pets
The Girls

Katherine Payran Corso Children
Saying Goodbye To Papa As He Leaves For Afghanistan

Dorrine G. Guinane Children
I Love Water Skiing

Jessica Jordan People
Mirror

Jennifer Brooke Erickson Travel
Strip

Nina Elizabeth Schultz Nature
Unlikely Neighbors

Melissa Lee Gerhardt Children
Just Like Daddy

Danny R. Barkhouse
Nature
Sunset On Salt Spring

Steve Miller
Nature
After The Storm

Mark John Kopczewski
Children
Georgia On My Mind

Robert Wiley
Nature
Colors Galore

Janet Lynne Yacino
Animals/Pets
Puppy Love

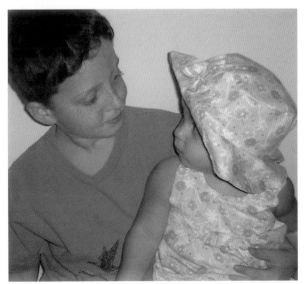

Jenny Pina
Children
A Picture Is Worth A Thousand Words

Holly C. Massie　　　　　　　　　　　　Children
New Cousin

Jose Carlos Mota　　　　　　　　　　　　People
Mena

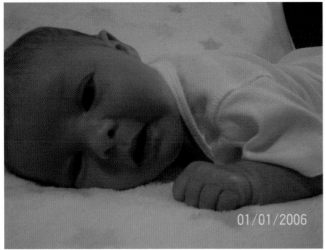

01/01/2006

Astra Star Adams　　　　　　　　　　　　Children
Beautiful Baby

Justina Litteral　　　　　　　　　　　　People
Untitled

Susan Fay Cornell　　　　　　　　　　　　Nature
Beach Creatures

Chelsea Schwartz　　　　　　　　　　　　People
Mistletoe

Catherine Dang   Animals/Pets
Minnie Penny

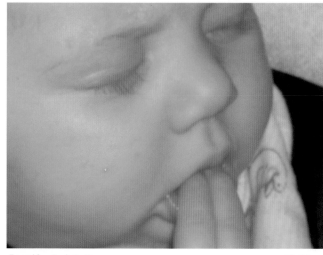

Jennifer Leigh Brown   Children
Close-Up

Chad Cebulski   Children
Gracie

Gladys I. Athill   Nature
After The Storm

Lori Teather James   Other
Best Friends

Karen K. Maxon   Children
Carter

Heather Rea Zebeck   Children
Santa's Little Helper

Mary Susan Troublefield   Children
Innocence

Mary R. White   Children
I'm Going To Tell Mama On You; It's Mine!

Scott Alan Sutton   Nature
Waterfall At Ricketts Glen State Park

Alan Michael Torok-Both   Action
Horsepower

Ray Flood   People
Siesta

Debby L. Carnathan   Other
Night At The Fair

Jessie Wolfe   Children
Jayda's Birthday Cake

Eric Provost   Children
Thirsty

Natallie Ortiz   Animals/Pets
My Cat Stole My Homework

Charity Weber   Children
Fun In The Ball Pit

Aliya M. Schlea   Animals/Pets
Honolua Bay Dolphins

Fleur Guibovich   Nature
Beautiful In Pink

Alan M. Lynch   Travel
Respect

Michael L. Chuma   Travel
The Beauty Of Silence — Lassen National Park, California

Gareth Walters   Nature
Ah, Life

Jaime K. Pahler   Animals/Pets
African Elephant In Kenya

Anthony Michael Gemus   Other
Reflections

Karen Lyndoe Schultz   Animals/Pets
Norton Cheese

Lora B. Brown   Children
Back Porch

William L. DuPree   Nature
Dragonfly

Jennifer Nichole Aitken   Nature
Glory Afternoon

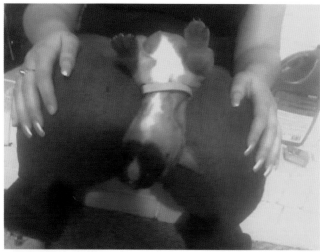

Jessica Marie Jeffers   Animals/Pets
Lazy Blade

Meloney Ballew   Animals/Pets
Samson Claus

James Howard Ward   Nature
Blue Garden

Jess Ann Morgan   Nature
Gone (What Wonder)

Steven Wade Myers   Children
Bubblicious

Chelsea Hull   Travel
Great Silhouette

Peggy Ann Moyers   Animals/Pets
Susey Q

Debra Ann Spencer   Children
King Catch

Linda Viramontes   Nature
Crosses In The Light

Amy Wence   Animals/Pets
Mandarinfish On Mushroom Polyps

Larry R. Parks   Nature
Storm Clouds

Eyreka Cummings   People
Friends For Life!

David W. Lamb   Nature
Things Are Looking Up

Sean Peterson   Nature
Morning Glory

Jeannie Marie Baczek   Animals/Pets
First Snow

Gary Edward Looker   Other
A Grand Pace

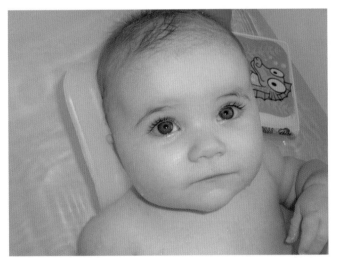

Nicole Elizabeth Richardson   Children
My Beautiful Bright Eyes

Marie T. Baldwin   Nature
Red Tulips In Spring

Andrew Houston-McMillan   Nature
The Ring Of Hope

Neil Michael Smail   Animals/Pets
Desire

Michelle A. Greco Children
Trust Me

William Colt Chandler Animals/Pets
Making Way

Karelle Marie Locay Animals/Pets
The Wonderful Lucy

Fred Rosenberg Travel
Welcoming The Day — Bridgehampton, New York

Colleen Elizabeth Kenny Travel
Golden Gate

June M. L. Gooch Animals/Pets
Happy Green Lizard

Megan McAdams   Children
Sweet

Teri Lynn Roper   Nature
A New Mexico Sunset

Bette Ann Newman   Other
Old Glory In The Sunset

Elizabeth Riley   Animals/Pets
I Miss You, Kelly

Kimberly Lynnette Amburn   Nature
Sunrise On Sanibel Island

Tommy E. Duckworth   Travel
Highway 66

Michelle Lee Nichols   Other
Smoky Mountain Cabin

Cyndi Ann Skidmore   Nature
Serenity

Kathy S. Cohen   Nature
Family Outing

Gordon Wendell Merrill   Nature
Spider On A Web

Shane Dean Halliday   Animals/Pets
Poster Cat

Karen Diane Hanes   Portraiture
The Perfect Dress

Remi Syrenne   Nature
Prairie Cascade

Melinda Marie Antonowicz   Nature
New Hampshire Fall

Trenton Micheal Johnson   Other
Undercover Operations

Michael Joseph Maccaro   Nature
Canyon De Chelly

Cheryl C. Hall   Nature
God's Window

Thomas R. Martinelli   Children
Base Talk

Rick Lee Kendle Animals/Pets
Where's The Banana?

Vivian Gutierrez Animals/Pets
Cat's Meow

Margaret Anne Redrup Animals/Pets
If We Could Talk To The Animals

Bradley W. Myers Travel
London At Dusk

Mark Anthony Francis Animals/Pets
Spider Monkey

Karen Lynn LeClair Children
Twins

Nicola M. Stith Other
Carrot Love

Nikki Joy Aguero Children
Sisterly Love

Molly Bean People
Working In The Coal Mine

Shannon Connolly People
Classic Beauty

Raul Arzola Animals/Pets
Boo

Lauren Palmer Travel
Hopeful Wondering

Wim T. Tel Travel
Watching The Water Boil

Travis Gibbs Nature
California Coast

Elizabeth Mary Nott Nature
San Francisco Sunset

Andrea Mary Compagnino Nature
Yellow Tulips

Emily Lentz Nature
On Top Of The World

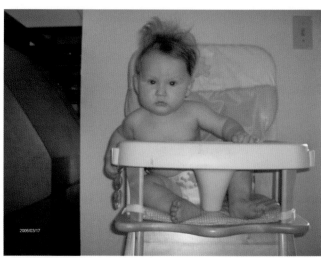

Crystal Adams Children
Chloe Lynn

Chelsea Dove Children
Snow Angel

Gerald Lee Tuttle Portraiture
Reflections

Phillip Cooley Nature
African Daisy

Tamara L. Knapp Children
Jones Lake 2005

Renate Buck Nature
Adirondack Winter

Chris Hoffman Sports
Dylan Jump

Paul Jared Pekrkins   Nature
River's Stepping Stones

William Shawn Breze   People
Dirt Curtain

Alex Hernandez   Action
Rockin' Out

Heather Anne Zarnow   Nature
Lightning Off Of Hilton Head Island

Edward J. Westall   Portraiture
Contemplating Life

Curtis Braxton Hardin   Nature
In Need Of Wanderlust

Mark Poppe   Nature
A Reflection

Kenya Janice Henry   People
The Girls

Adrian Whereat   Other
Sunset Stone Throw

Russ Harpring   Other
Snow Bridge

Susan Juggert   Nature
Simply Rose

Lynee Meverden   Animals/Pets
Gazing

Charee Spencer   Children
Summer Days

Corey Scott Arter   Nature
Contemplation Of A Dream

George Felipe Nunes   Children
Yin Yang

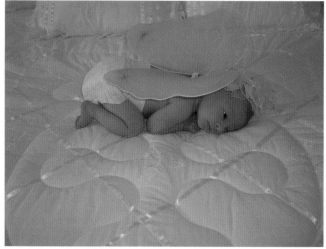

Kimberly Dawn Boyer   Children
Mallory In Fairyland

Andy Todd Maben   Travel
Jail In The 1800s

Noel Johnson   Animals/Pets
Kiki

Tiffany Brooke Niewohner　　　　　　Children
Playing Peek

Suzanne Rohrer　　　　　　Animals/Pets
Annie

Daren Maloy　　　　　　Nature
The Lone Cypress Of Monterey

Eleanor Parr-DiLeo　　　　　　People
Best Friend

Ronnie L. Esparza　　　　　　Animals/Pets
Rainy Day

Catherine Anne Newman　　　　　　Nature
Reflections

Marisela Pena People
My Thinking

Kim Rodney Langmaid People
Vanuatu's Children

Eric Norman Anderson Nature
God's Natural Artwork

Robert V. Eloe Nature
New Day

Ryan Tack Animals/Pets
Face To Face

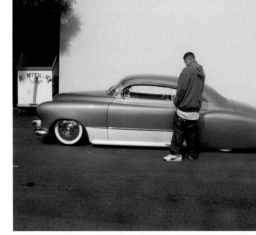

David Arthur VanDyke People
Low Down

Gloria J. Nelson   Children
Mother's Loving Kiss

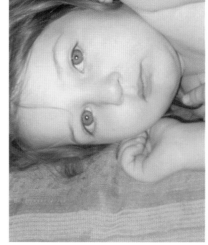

Hannah Marie Roberts   Children
Amariah Grace

Mary M. Brennan   Nature
Raindrops

Wendy Rene Thurlow   Travel
Boy With Dog In Costa Rica

Mary Elizabeth Chaney   Animals/Pets
Catnap

Laura St. Pierre   Nature
On A Journey To Nowhere

Teresa S. Ortega   Nature
Standing Proud And Tall

Tegan Moyer   Children
Hanging Out With The Birds

Karina Mott   Animals/Pets
Bella

Rachel Anne Powers   Nature
Leafy Shadows

Andres M. Gutierrez   Action
San Francisco

Renee Tufaro   Animals/Pets
My Peanut

Dmitriy Protassov   People
Veronica

Robin A. Bauder   Nature
Just Like Me, Woodpecker

Christine Questore   Animals/Pets
Pounce

Pantelis Anastasios Korovilas   Other
Through My Eyes

Caylon Lawrence Hackwith   Other
Rear View Mirror

Dustin Lewis   Nature
Indonesian Sunrise

Jonathan Elizondo   Travel
Ellam

Candise Steven Griffin   Nature
Beyond Beauty

Katherine G. Hupp   Animals/Pets
Puppy Love

Janet De La Cruz   Nature
Mt. Rushmore Trees

Eddie Sanchez   People
Watch Your Brother

Lara Bee   Nature
Saluting Tulip, Nature's Mishaps

Eric J. Acker Children
Eva Rosa

Sharon Ann Lyle Nature
Autumn At The Lake

Adrian Nebozuk Nature
Osprey Catch Of The Day

Sae Oh Children
Crouching Hannah, Hidden Princess

Ramesh Shanmugasundaram Children
New Generation

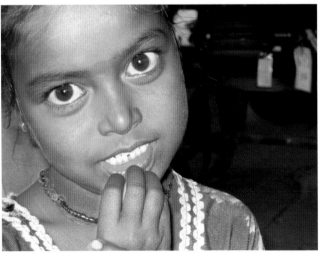

Kathleen A. Marshall People
Beggar Girl

Nora Lynn Martin Animals/Pets
Portrait Of A Pug

Amber Leigh Howard Children
Heading West

Katie Boyce Animals/Pets
You've Got Frog!

K.J. Velasquez Nature
Day's End — Sandia Mountains, New Mexico

Elissa Guynup Children
Bare Footin'

Alene T. Rambsel Animals/Pets
Stevie

Med Myra Miranda Frani   Children
Say Cheese!

Addie Colleen Ferry   Animals/Pets
Mockingbird After A Cool Spring Rain

Tina Andersen   People
Should I, Or Shouldn't I?

Angele Badeaux James   Children
Sibling Love

Juan Carlo Bermudez   Children
God Fire Best Wishes

Melvin Wong   Travel
Venice Of The Orient

Kimberly Ann Ball People
Larry Reed

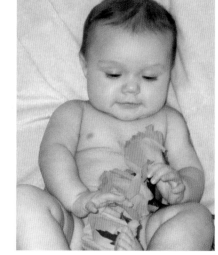

Jenna L. Musil Children
Abbygail Rose

Pat A. Silva Children
Morning Ride

Tyro Lee Nature
Morning Sun

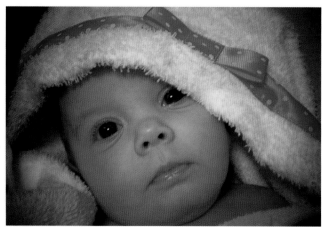

Chelsye Jo Graham Children
Chelsye Jo Graham

Zaida Rita Borelli Travel
Gentoo Penguin Feeding Her Chick — Antarctica

Dora Na   Animals/Pets
Early Morning

Lounise Percinthe   Animals/Pets
Bruce And Erica

James Arthur Presnell   Travel
Somewhere In Time

Cari Oveta Fonseca   Nature
What A Sunset

Sandie Lora Scott   Portraiture
Waiting To Love You

Debbie Peterson   Children
Little One

Nassara Sloan   Animals/Pets
Sox And Kitty

Monica Hurley   Animals/Pets
Time To Swim

Crystal Harrison   Children
You Know He's Tired

Steven Spicknall   Travel
Seattle 2005

Bob Lipiro   Nature
Sanibel After The Storm

Rebecca Hansen   Animals/Pets
Chaser

Wallace Edwin Moore Animals/Pets
Total Concentration

Mai Sao Vang People
Never Again

Kate Molloy Animals/Pets
Puppy's Hiding Place

Andrew Richard Pedersen Travel
Archways Of The Alhambra In Granada, Spain

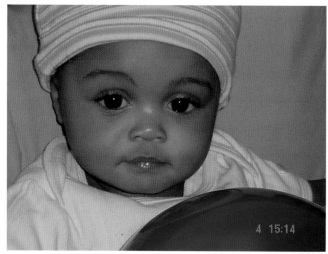

Pearle J. G. Armstrong Children
It's Not Your Birthday; It's My Balloon

Ivan Berkowitz Nature
A Glorious Sunset Across Trout Lake!

Eduardo Frias-Etayo People
On Site Tailoring

Jon Cutler Travel
Learning To Fly

Rachel Red Children
Peek-A-Boo

Courtney Bowman Other
Stairs

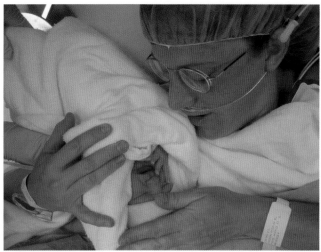

Eric Gephart Children
First Touch

Randy Christopher Sparcello Animals/Pets
Love, In Memory Of Butch (March 1997–December 2005)

Peter Ralph Cammarata   Travel
The Gondolier

Susan Rodriguez   Humor
Look, Mom, No Heads!

Katherine M. Mathews   Animals/Pets
Pet Me

Melanie Goslin   Nature
Hiking In Tarrywile Park, Danbury, Connecticut

Cristy Marie Felix   Nature
White Serenity

Lorraine Story-Holloway   Nature
Hello

Cindy Lafleur Animals/Pets
Dad And Daisy

Karen D. Clayton Portraiture
Fountain At The Ravines

Kirk Pierce Children
My Little Cowboy

Chanthachone Tui Humor
He Had No Idea!

Megan Commander Children
Day At The Beach

Peter Charles Dahm Sports
A View From The Green

Jeffrey McLaughlin Travel
Flight line

Janette Ann Hoover Nature
Sunflower Sky

James C. Morgan Children
Sparkling Curiosity

Dorian Johnson Travel
On The Road In Iraq

John Andrew LaGrega Other
Fire Island Lighthouse

Janel Lynn Rankin Nature
Pink Roses

John E. Dunn People
Curious Christmas

Gabrian Holloway Children
Me And My Own

Matthew Lorenz Nature
Northwest Fork Of The Alligator River

Crystal Lyons Bateman Animals/Pets
Too Cute

Jack Lagomarsino Other
Seltzer And Lime

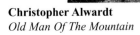

Christopher Alwardt Nature
Old Man Of The Mountain

Ivel Paroulek People
Eighteen And Alive

Geraldine Ludas Animals/Pets
Thirsty

David R. Vanasse People
Serenity

Marjorie Louise Minyard Children
Lauren

Kay Howard Animals/Pets
Mmm, That Was Good!

Kami Michelle Periman Animals/Pets
Miikka

Carrie Lee O'Neal   Other
An Inspiration

Wendy P. Gift   Nature
Tulip Beauty

Darryl James Vega   Nature
Wintry Day

Heather Eileen Carlson-Acton   Nature
Birthday Rose

Chris Johnson   Animals/Pets
Help Us!

James Gerald Acton   Nature
Cochrane Hay Field

Dustin A. DeBoer   Animals/Pets
Trail Work 245

Lyle Don Dejmal   Nature
Kansas Tree

Jo Ann Fagan   Animals/Pets
I Can Fly!

Daniel B. McNeill   Travel
The Pastel Colors Of St. Martin

Deonna Lynn Moore   Other
Fire And Steel

Delia C. Krieger   Nature
Tropical Travel In Hawaii

Gregg David Janecky Travel
Deception Pass

Stephen J.B. Drake Nature
Mirror, Mirror

Bernie Mansuetti Nature
Eyes Of The Forest

Gabra Sutricia Bennett Children
Daddy Buried Me In Hawaii

Kimberly Ann Jackson Children
Bubbles

Kim M. Harrington Children
Reindeer Marie

Brian Arthur Biedugnis Nature
Rocky Mountain Sunset

Carol Catizone Nature
Light Of Day

DeWayne Mark LeBleu Animals/Pets
Lovers On My Front Porch

Colleen Kwiecinski Animals/Pets
Kasia

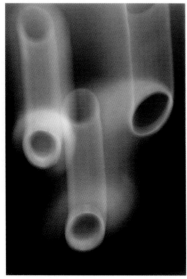

Molly Starr Lucas Other
Voices

David Eugene Lewis Action
Three Rivers Of Old

Ian Ashcroft   Animals/Pets
Silent Love

Kerry Wargo   Animals/Pets
Lazy Leopard — Botswana

Phyllis Mae Wright   Humor
The Aliens Are Coming

Amber Lyn Simmons   Children
In The Pumpkin Patch

Marla Kathleen Raines   Children
Blue Eyes

Crystal Lynn Sullivan   Animals/Pets
Liber-Poochi

Joseph Daniel Graber　　　　　　　Children
Tessa Having A Cozy Moment

Alannah Del Reid　　　　　　　Children
Taylor

Julie Childers　　　　　　　Other
Relaxing, Viewing The Beautiful Turquoise Ocean

Brigitte L. Burstein　　　　　　　Animals/Pets
Nuggles

Deborah Palmer　　　　　　　Animals/Pets
Smile, Pretty Kid

Jessie L. Malcolm　　　　　　　Children
Beach Baby

Rebecca Ann Shields   Other
Circles Of Joy

Joseph Patrick Adrian   Animals/Pets
Love My Lamb

Gloria Sharber   Animals/Pets
Maui

Craig Burton   Nature
Mountain Stream

Robert Marshall Evasic   Animals/Pets
Murial's Close-Up

Cassandra O'Brian   Travel
Ft. McClary, Maine

David Miranda
Mist On Mammoth

Nature

Christina Rose Parks
Birds In Flight

Nature

Antonia V. Atherton
Close Encounter

Animals/Pets

Neal S.C. Martyn
Star At The Beach

Animals/Pets

Ashlee Nichole Miller
The Funny Me!

Portraiture

Brenda Gail Anderton
Special Moments

People

Theodore Thomas Smith
Peek-A-Boo!
Animals/Pets

Connice Chrystal Lagace
The Jaguar
Animals/Pets

Ben Edward Boutin
A Day At The Beach
Action

Christina Dawn Beverage
Ocracoke, North Carolina
Travel

Debbie A. Witmer
A Rough Night
Animals/Pets

Kati Aileen Corbett
Beautiful Sunset
Nature

Cindy Jean Morrison Nature
Scenery

Nina L. Cansler Nature
Sunrise

Elmer W. Parker Animals/Pets
Mountain Lion At Caldwell Zoo

Jerusha Ann Sutton Children
Olivia, The Little Poser

Elaine M. Fournier Children
Baby On Beach

Krystal Rose Kelly Animals/Pets
Mystical

Richard V. Laton   Animals/Pets
Cats

Stacy Justice   Children
Cutie Pie Julie

Carol J. McSherry   Nature
Flutter By Ford

Ewa Bednarska   Nature
Impression

Dave Andrew Cumming   Nature
Friends At The Grand Canyon

Dianne Wennick   Children
Steam Room Children's Style

Angela Dwyer   Animals/Pets
Maddox And Baby Squirrel

Derek Thomas Armstrong   Travel
Ethiopian Countryside

Terri M. Palazzolo   Animals/Pets
Finding Me

Brian Donahoo   Nature
Bridal Veil In Ice

Chelsie Rodriguez   People
Get Back Up With A Smile!

Chris A. Banta   Animals/Pets
Cool Dog

James Francis Bennett
White Sand, New Mexico

Nature

Nicole Villafane
Hawaii

Travel

Melissa Victoria Hetelekidis
Dressed To Kill

Children

Tracey Jean Henson
Tom

People

Donald B. Humphries
My Favorite Witch

Children

Rhonda S. Taylor
I'm Sitting Pretty

Children

Deana S. Devries   Children
That's My Daddy!

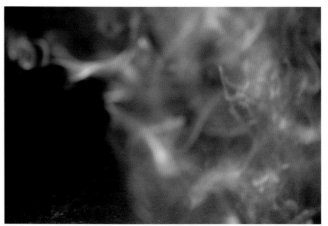

Tammy Michelle Pierson   Other
Ghost Of St. Augustine

Catherine Susanne Dall   Nature
Reflection

Vickie King   Nature
Springtime Velvet

Matt Kronshage   Nature
Sunset

Christine Noel Fusselman   Animals/Pets
Non Conformist

Jose Renteria Castro Humor
Happy Little Boy

Howard Roy Yingling Animals/Pets
Speed Limit?

Andree Resurreccioin People
Aly And Dre

Sarah-Jane Laubscher Travel
Sunrise In Symmetry

Meghan C. Wright Nature
God's Beauty

Susan Jean Freyermuth Children
Innocent Emily

Vladimir Braslavsky   Portraiture
Tarzan

Inna Shenker   Nature
My Snowy Day — February 12, 2006

Jerry Valentin   Nature
Ligthhouse At Cabo Rojo

Morgan Paige Wessel   Children
Curious

Chris Beers   Animals/Pets
My Puppy Chillin'

Melissa Kaye Kranz   Children
I'll Be Safe In Here!

Sherry Laughhunn Children
You Found Me!

Anne-Marie Celine Pambrun Nature
Peaceful Morning

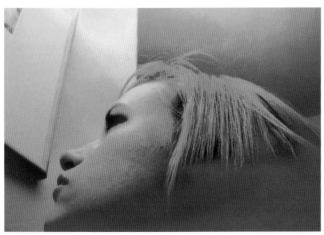

Kaelie Ripple Portraiture
Thinking

Greg John Mutton Nature
Last Light

Thomas R. Jones Animals/Pets
Jasper Looking At Reindeer

Desirae Gayle Brown Animals/Pets
Afternoon Graze

Billie Dozer Animals/Pets
My Smiling Tank

Beata Zera People
Myself

Lindsey Michelle Beason Nature
The Face In The Sky

Kristi Lynn Rogers Nature
Osprey In Flight

Benjamin Bonfanti Other
Reflections

William Kyle Miller Travel
Statue Of Liberty

Jim Stevenson   Nature
Snow Trees

Christine L. Armstrong   Humor
Look At That Mane

Shannon Plummer   Animals/Pets
Elephant Mirror

Tamera Lynn Kavouras   Nature
Morning Moon

Rochelle Meek   Animals/Pets
Leave Me Alone!

Carol Ann Sullivan   Nature
Calming Evening

Aida Fuersich Nature
The Sky Is The Limit

Diane Klevecka Nature
Divine Garden

William Allan Prante Animals/Pets
Who Stole My Candy?

Carl Steven Donze Children
Bubble Girl

Lisa Kay Wimberly Travel
Beauty Trapped In Time

Rae Lynn Allen Children
Camera Shy

Carol E. Reyna   Other
Pretty In Pink

Jenny Connolly   Children
China Doll

Kalei Amion   Travel
Kalei

Nancy Kelly   Nature
Bonanza Day Lily

Angela Nolan   Other
Afghanistan Medevac

Rose Leon   Nature
Cactus

M. Skrysak   Children
In Awe

Mary Kay Blosser   Other
Tranquility

Chris Thomas   Travel
Rails To Heaven

Sandi Sexton   Animals/Pets
Lex Boy

Hal Eric Richendrfer   Animals/Pets
Ever Vigilant

Johanna Maria Crookston   Children
Georgia

Alicia Ann Buist   Children
Water Play

Jennifer Dawn Marr   Children
Alyssa Sleeping

Dea Francine Mcbride   Animals/Pets
Smile

Joe Vivo   Other
Snow Shadows

Jillian Marie Kinn   Travel
Florence

Amy M. Booth   Children
Smiling Pretty

Chris J. De Bruyckere   Children
Halloween Monkey

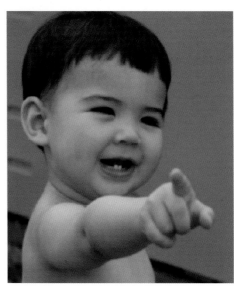

Linda Abadie   Children
To The Point

Wilma Tryka   Animals/Pets
Just Horsing Around

Christina Louise Danner   Children
Static Fun

Wendy Marie Cunningham   Travel
End Of Day

Stephanie M. Gladwell   Animals/Pets
Cuddles

Julie Maxey Dale People
The New Pope — November 2005

Pam B. Abeling Children
Kasey At Play

Russ Ebsen Action
Taming The Beast

Shari Mae Breen Animals/Pets
I'm Ready

Tami S. Jones Nature
Butterfly

Paula Irene Westberry Nature
Lone Tree

Amy Robl
Muddy Pup
Animals/Pets

Kerri L. Law
Of Cats And Bears
Animals/Pets

Marius Baciu
Red Sky In Alberta Oil Field
Nature

Amanda Rae Moore
Hangin' Out
Animals/Pets

Julie Milan
Evening Reflection
Nature

Adam Ouahmane
Alley
Other

Zahin Singh   Nature
The Calm

Robyn Alison Kightly   Nature
Gumnuts

Courtnie Robertson   Action
Cheerleading

Susan L. Beddows   Nature
Hypnotic

Vicky Williams   Animals/Pets
My Cat's Pose

Walter J. Fontaine   Other
Mount Washington

Deborah Need   Animals/Pets
Skunky

Loraine Paul   Children
Come On Grandma, Go In The Woods With Us, Please

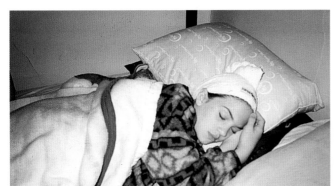

Bonnie Matelyan   Children
My Poor Head!

Joe Curry   Nature
Life In Bloom

Marilyn Eberle   Children
Hold On

Allison Russo   Travel
New York At Night

Ann Ora Troxler Other
Phantom Rider

Verda Swartentruber Portraiture
Life Is Great

Charlotte S. McCaslin Travel
Heidelberg Castle

Mayfield Nitzel Portraiture
Partner

Jo Anna L. Reister Travel
The Hidden Cove — Big Sur Coastline, California

Joan Wingo People
Grin Of Insecurity

Jane Marie Heflin   Nature
Serenity

Melissa Ann Roney   Children
I Still See You!

Jana LaVonne Hartley   Children
I Do Believe I Can Fly

Lael Rogers   Children
Bu, The Rose Baby

Dawn Renee Weisheim   Children
Mason Sleeping

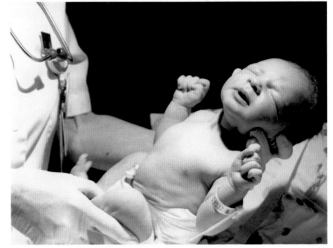

Cynthia Anne Hammond   People
A New Beginning

Laura Schuler   Nature
Opening Up To The World

Katie Diane Roberts   Children
Blue Steel

Theresa Marie Salo   People
Chrome

Bruce Bruce Hopkins   Nature
State Of Mind

Katherine P. Joyce   Children
Hey, Mom, Look At My Stick!

Cindy Dawn Laverdiere   Children
I Want To Party With Grandma

Susan K. DeVries
After The Storm

Nature

Sylvia M. Westenbroek
Iguana

Animals/Pets

Sarah Jane O'Neill
Two Branch Island Spring Snow

Nature

Brent Clarke
The Pond

Nature

Patsy Ann Lockhart
Sitting Pretty

Children

Harry M. Fraser
Molly On The Shore

Children

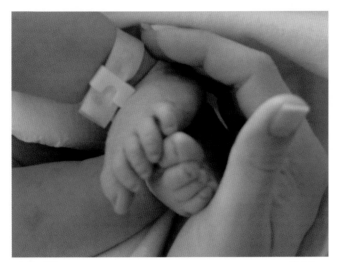

Kelly Glines   Children
A Mother's Touch

Tyrone C. Trotman   Nature
Off Into The Sunset

Jason Micheal Massey   Portraiture
Lost In A Picture

Kyle Patrick Dehn   Nature
Early Morn

Rick Arellano   Nature
Heavenly Shine

Danielle Lee Davis   Nature
Dog Days Of Summer

Ginger deVegh   Animals/Pets
Sleeping Lola

Rebecca Murphy   Other
Urban Angel

Tina Michele Hostetler   Nature
Florida Skies

Myrek R. Bialuski   Portraiture
Days Gone By

Randy E. Alvarado   Children
I Want To Be A Cowboy

Ashley Marie Maris   Travel
Flying High

Michelle Filpus   Travel
London's Roar

Cheryl K. Gauthier   People
Just A Cutie

Linda Kay Truman   Children
Jacob Nolan

William Eric Fahey   Nature
Relaxation On A Rainy Day

Carl Philip Hall   People
Mum And Dad

Hina Malik   Travel
Rainbow Of Life

Sara Cambria Nature
Perspective

Jill E. Leonard Animals/Pets
I Want My Bath

Joshua Lake Travel
Sunset In Michigan

Josefina Holguin Gerende Travel
Misty Nights

Todd Becker Other
City Hall

Opal Trajano Burgess Children
Be Mine

Yvone Flatter　　　　　　　　　　　Nature
Sunset

Sonia Millan　　　　　　　　　　　Portraiture
Speechless

Ashley Morgan Malcho　　　　　　Nature
Bay Of Fundy At Low Tide

Emily Kathleen Williams　　　　　Nature
Captivating Sky

John Edward Norcom　　　　　　　Other
Blue Moon

William Orts　　　　　　　　　　　Nature
Star Bright

James Richard Stratton
Taking One For The Team

Sports

Tia Guenther
Maui Harbor Sunrise

Nature

Raymond Edward Kinsaul
Lifting Off And Heading Home

Action

George Jerdee
Mini Hulk

Children

Dena Lee Moran
Who's The Big Dog Here?

Animals/Pets

Samantha J. Rabel
Freedom

Travel

Cheryl Lynn O'Neal People
True Blue

John Samuel Feiser Nature
Summer Day

Deborah Verwey Nature
Timeless Tranquility

Christopher Joesph Greaves Nature
Rocky Wave

Adam Seth Esacove Children
Picnic Blanket

Connie Dae Nahalka Animals/Pets
Stage Mother And The Foo-Foo Sisters

Jyl M. Lauer Children
Missy In Vegas

Nicholas Matthew Rose Animals/Pets
Wildlife At The Airport

Marcia J. Brennan Children
Aspiring Sea Captain

Elian Velazquez Nature
Puerto Rico Sunset

Chuck W. Wooley Children
In Due Time

Helen Drew Animals/Pets
First Friends

Linda M. MacIntyre   Nature
Hanna Park At Dusk

Emmalyn Carter German   Animals/Pets
Rainy Day Cat

Dawn Marie Silverio   Travel
Ocho Rios, Jamaica

Ron Loving   Nature
Winter Time

Warren Bruce Mackie   Other
Limu Ship

Natalya Shabalinsky   Nature
Beautiful Age

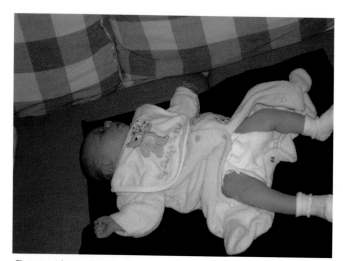

George Alexander Davison
All Tuckered Out

Children

Craig Robert Somerville
Lady's Finger

Nature

Linda Sue Diehl
Amanda

Children

Paul Leroy Christensen
Mud Pies

People

Cletus Lee Lampard
Sunset In Aruba

Travel

Ronald Thomas Welty Sr.
Dusk Fire

Nature

Marlene Marie Toledo
Children
Thinking Of You

Taylor Marie Kensel
Other
Spectrum

Brenda Arlene Kifer
Nature
Untitled

Martin Huminski
Travel
No Ending

Lisa Noakes
Nature
Destination

Brande Michelle Willis
Children
The Dirt Road

Aletha Leann Zsido Travel
Tibetan Woman At Prayer Wheel

Christine Rubina Farmilo Travel
Serenity

Shira Boker People
Eye

Ana Luiza Batista Children
Bird In Hand

Carole Susan Clark Children
Tired Elf

Danielle M. Meadors Animals/Pets
Best Friends

Sandi Kay Brown   Animals/Pets
Happy Hour

Sara Allison Skubal   Other
Remembering

Laura Snavely   Other
Freedom

Jenny Lynn Nelson   Children
The Cutest Baby!

Wendy Wayne Angle   Animals/Pets
Thunder Baby

Dan DeBoer   Travel
Helsingborg Sunset

Dave John Battjes   Other
Empty

Treva Pletscher   Animals/Pets
Ever Watchful

Vurlma Rae Coulter   Nature
Las Cruces Sunset

Linda Underwood   Portraiture
Waiting For The Next Dance

D. Bartkow   Other
Our Creator's Touch

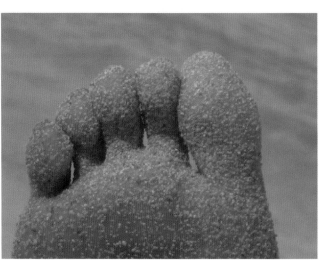

Taylor Skelton   Travel
A Day At The Beach

Deena J. Neville   Animals/Pets
I Want To Go Outside, Mom!

Aleksandra Furmanskaya   Children
The Happy Baby

Ron Durbin   Children
Bath Time

Krista Lee Wilson   Nature
Pagoda

Linda E. Bader   Nature
Beauty In The Woods

Candace Melanie Beckwith   Children
Big Feet

Dianna M. Sigler Children
Learning To Ski From The Shore

03/15/2006

Beverly Darlene Miller People
Kissing Cousins

Nina J. Pelliccione Children
Aussie Kid

Raye L. Berg-Nava Children
Too Cute

Todd Deblieck Other
The Desert Through The Eyes Of A Marine

Laura Elizabeth Henderson Travel
Walkway Through The Past

Brandi Zeiber
My Little Angel

Children

Douglas J. Inkol
A Day In Saint Tropez

People

Robert Lemaster
Sealed With A Kiss

Animals/Pets

Ralph A. Monte
Manhood

People

Kristy Hernandez
Blowing Kisses

Children

Tara Leigh Dallas
The London Eye

Humor

Barbara Vickrey   Children
Wow, I Love Christmas!

Shaughn Crawford   People
The Chosen One

Michelle M. Martin   Children
Chocoholic In The Making

Heather J. Pitts   Nature
Backyard Bee

Casey Lee Baynum   Children
Little Secrets

Craig John Boundy   Nature
Morning Billabong

Tywonna LoQuice Wright   Portraiture
Light

Christine Lynn Opila-May   Nature
Grasshopper In Bertha's Garden

Teresa Macri   Children
Grandma's Pride

Natasha Torres   People
Don't I Look Like A Model?

Kaitlyn Wright   Children
My Sweet Baby Boy

Collin Fossen   Nature
No Skins Today

Terri J. Corley   Children
All Boy

Wilmarie D. Newton   Travel
El Morro

Penny Vess   Children
The Gift Of Hula

Raj Singh   Other
Brooklyn's Bridge

Timothy Michael Johnson   Children
I'm Sitting

Rosalie Sabarese   People
Little Girl Lost

Julia Diane Allen
Sunday Morning

Other

Richard Casamento
Journey's End

Nature

Barbara A. Besteni
Ronda Serenity

Travel

Hunter Bosley
Isolation Verde

Nature

Olivia Mae Brune
Who Says Pit Bulls Are Mean?

Animals/Pets

Bridgette A. Hurley
Springtime Renewal

Nature

David J. Dadisman Nature

Before The Storm

Mary J. Wigham People

I Love You, Mommy

Shannon Jennifer Bettis Nature

Under Tree Looking Up

Conni Ann Harblin People

Hands Of Time

Barbara Mellinger Animals/Pets

Please Play With Me

David Alan Schauer Action

Fly High

Shellie Irene Hickok
Sunset In Alaska

Nature

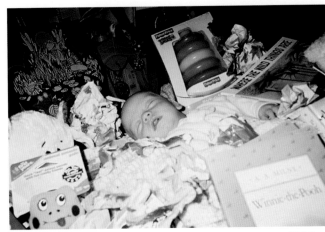

Jennifer Lynn Trissel
My First Christmas

Children

Elizabeth A. Hess
Hangin' Out With Big Brother

Children

Patty Lynn Mellor
Evening Sky

Nature

Robert John Zirpoli
Morning Nets

Other

Thomas Eugene Tramel
Sunset Highway

Nature

Diane Ruth Blonski-Kavosick   Animals/Pets
Frisbee Friends

Karen Tomczak   Animals/Pets
Santa Bud-D

Anna M. Russo   People
Breakfast

Georgia L. Roy   Children
Happiest Kids On The Planet

Patti Sheldon   Nature
Paradise In Orange

Jarmila Stupka   Children
Caroline Petra O'Hagan

Alison Leigh Swartz   Portraiture
Logic

Constance Patricia French   Animals/Pets
Mums The Word

Luis Fung   Other
Harmony Of Things

James Douglas Shields   Children
Young Girl And Grandmother

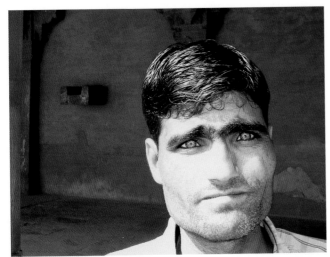

Gonzalo A. Perez   People
Indian Man

Karen Roberts   Animals/Pets
'Hare' Today, Gone Tomorrow

Morgan Brooke Zielinski   Animals/Pets
Best Friends

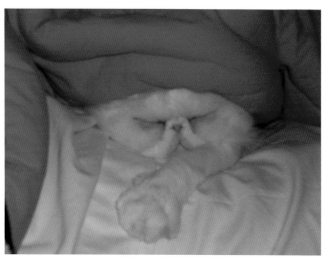

Ashley Akins   Animals/Pets
Sleeping Beauty

Paul James Grainger   Animals/Pets
Oh, Mum

Cantriece Shavelle Kelley   People
You're Never Too Old For A Push

Darlene Jewel Tejada   Children
Life Is Fun At Two

Travis Ray Hammond   Nature
Hanging Fog

Laurie A. Pallot
People
Hitching A Ride

Angela Varouhakis
Travel
I Love Aussie Beaches!

Steve Emrich
People
Don't Bite Off More Than You Can Chew

Clarence John Snyder Jr.
Other
Star Rising

Anthony James Buckland
Nature
Ocean View

Lisa Marie Brown
People
Shawna Marie

Tom Staton
Open To All

Nature

Kristi Ann Daynes
Our Surprise Angel

Children

Jeanne Brunn
My Sweet Jada Boy

Animals/Pets

Dziyana Kubanina
Captivated

Children

Kathy Felts
A Drop Of Rain

Nature

James Walter Chernesky
After The Storm

Nature

Charles J. Perrin   People
Washington Beauty

Lisa Michelle Bowman   Nature
On Top Of The World

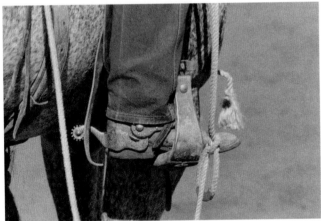

Jessica Jo Ulrich   Other
Spur

Kevin S. Mills   Nature
Mirror Image Of Lizard Pond

Jamie Marie Magruder   Nature
Snow In Spring

Jamie Sousa   Children
Have A Little Faith

James Paul Salay   People
Palm Head Dude

Charlotte Hooper   Nature
God's Grandeur

Cathy A. Smith   Children
Mr. GQ

Gail Schuck   Travel
Arizona In The Springtime

Darren William Murray   Animals/Pets
Lioness

Eileen R. Mason   Nature
My Secret Hideout

Melissa S. Ferretti   Children
Where's The Teeth?

Tina C. Callahan   Nature
Pure Of Heart

Yoseth Guerrero   Nature
Tranquility

George Constantinos Prasinos   Animals/Pets
Disgruntled Bee

Marta Louise Barth   Nature
Dragonfly

Amber Snodgrass   Animals/Pets
Gizmo

Kenneth Holliday   Nature
Thistle

Danette E. Shoemaker   Children
Freinds In Low Places

Anna Marie Moser   People
Lonely Rider

Kerry Ann Henwood   Children
Village Girl

Marvin Duane Ball   People
London Youth

Liz Slane   Children
My Baby

Lynn Michele Houston
The Beauty Of Mt. Emily

Nature

James Arthur Mullier
Can We Go, Please?

Children

Sonya Lynn Cates
Kisses

Children

Stephen Paul Weller
All Things Great And Small

Nature

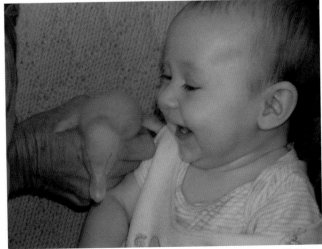

Chantry I. Leingang
Little Ducky

Children

Dawn M. Beasley
Herman

Animals/Pets

128

Cali A. Nellis Nature
Miniature Waterfall

Donna Trosper Other
The Union Of Hands

Jane Eileen Denton Travel
Lighthouse On Campo Bello Island, Canada

Katie Deming Other
Metallic Kaleidoscope

Christine Marie Beligan Other
Lake Tahoe Chase Building

Adjanys Santiago People
My Marilin

Christy Martin
Portraiture
Nana's Hat

Cameron Stewart Fox
Nature
Life Begins

Warwick Hudson Jones
Other
Hot Air Balloon

Gloria Jean Reynertson
People
Never Forgotten

Julie Anne Reitter
Nature
Bonfire

Stephen Ellis
Children
Autumn's Summer Vacation

Sandra Rae Leibig   Children
Happy Face

Kaci Nicole Norman   Nature
Tree Flower

Stan Richard   Travel
Pot O' Gold In Paradise

James Arthur Hannam   Nature
Sunset At White Sands

Christie Zielinski   Children
Emotions

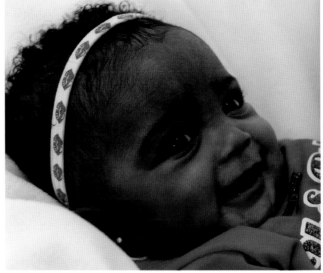

Amaya Donet Tillman   Children
My Princess In 2006

Tammy G. Brown   Nature
Angel In The Storm

Shawn Michael Walsh   Travel
Lonesome Trail

Misty M. Kuntschik   Children
Look At Me

Michael S. Copeland   Nature
Colorado

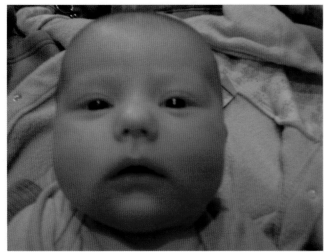

Tanya E. Justham   Children
What's Up?

Misty Lee Barnett   Children
A Birthday Party

Alex Christian Maisey
Reflections — Chile, South America

Nature

Marcia M. Gavin
Refreshing

Animals/Pets

Ana Rosario Tuma
Sunset

Nature

Valerie Griffiths
Betswy Coed

Travel

Monique Marie Bouthillier
Mom And Daughter

Children

Michelle Forbes
Blue Man At Covent Garden, United Kingdom

People

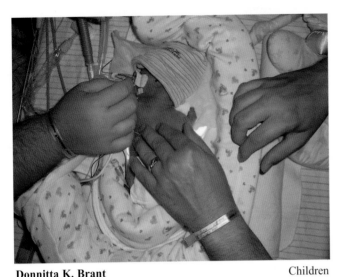

Donnitta K. Brant Children
God's Great Moments In Giving Life

Marjorie Louise Boozer Animals/Pets
Even They Can't Eat Just One

Tiffany Dickason Travel
Angel Of Heaven

Antonio Arroyo Animals/Pets
Untitled

Jenn Cantu Animals/Pets
Cuddling Sweethearts

Denise Lorraine Masonwells Animals/Pets
Baby Polar

Greg Paul Giordano People
I'm Ready!

Daphne Lukens Reed People
Music To Our Ears

Fred William Hess Animals/Pets
On Watch

Louis Michael Baskin Animals/Pets
Any More Foods

Theo Ochsenbein Animals/Pets
Ouch, What A Big World

Chris A. Warden Children
The Local Watering Hole!

Karen I. Wilson   People
After The Storm

Renee Young   Nature
I Got The Look

Susan M. Finn   Travel
Superbowl XL In Detroit

Peaches Kavanaugh   Nature
Beautiful Fall Day In Ohio

Warren H. Brown   Nature
Northern Lights — Quebec, Canada

Jessica Lynne Higgins   Animals/Pets
Sleepy

Riki Pope Nature
After The Rain

Anne Marie Lundberg Nature
Winter Morning At Canyon De Chelly

Meggan Ann Poynter Travel
Peek-A-Boo

Don F. Hershberger Nature
Oriental Lilies

Stacey Carey Children
Makenna

Amanda Karly Wishart Animals/Pets
I Don't Take Up Much Room

Dorothy Olais   Nature
Sky Contrast

Nurit Ana Moguilevsky   Travel
Gardel's Town

Jan Elizabeth Mitchell   Children
Oh, What A Feeling

Jane De Leon   Nature
Ice Teeth

William Morgenstein   Children
Grandkids Working

Dorothy Randell   Travel
Back In Time

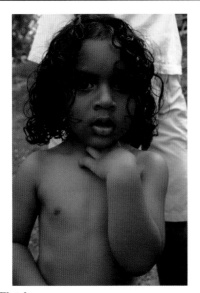

Jeff Dyvon Fletcher People
Pure Innocence

Kimberly Renee' Jauch Animals/Pets
Jazy's Snow Nose

Peter J. Scarfaro Sr. Nature
Sunset Over Weir Lake Road

Eric A. Kreuter Animals/Pets
Long Beard, Easy Rider

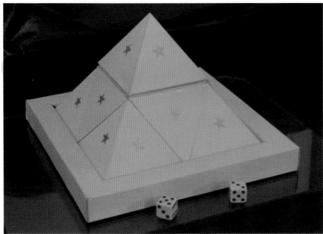

Martin Gravel Other
Magic Pyramid

Jennifer Hurd Animals/Pets
Ha!

Heather Kushner   Animals/Pets
A Nap With Her Baby

Leonard C. Marvicsin   Nature
A New Life

Joan Susan Delinski   Children
By The Beautiful Sea

G. Mckenzie   Nature
The Cherry Blossoms

Kristy Lee Watson   Children
Little Cowboy

Kelly Sue Snively   People
Old-Timer's Beauty

Kelly Garfield
Girl With Beard

Humor

Ken Moon
Peaceful Living

People

Jake Murphy
Jellyfish

Other

Jenny Lynn Herr
Irish Beach

Nature

Simeon Shane Norris
Sisters

People

Patricia Ann Bridges
Branson And Snuggles On The Farm

People

Madeline Fontenot   Children
Waiting

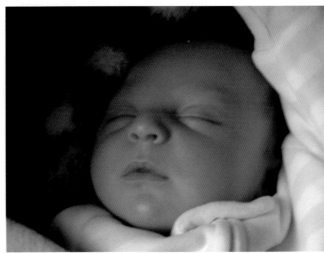

Heidi R. Collier   Children
Our Little Angel

Brian Thomas Murphy   Sports
Mark Redmen's Rehab

Jesse Campbell   Other
Faith

Janine V. Pendleton   Nature
Chesapeake Bay Bridge

Libby Gates   Animals/Pets
A Yawn Or Two

Paulette Marie Bullinger　　　　　　　　Children
Are You For Real?

Angel Delois Blue　　　　　　　　Nature
Over The River

Astrid Schalk　　　　　　　　Nature
Power Mountain

Grant Richard Watson　　　　　　　　Nature
Lightning Strikes

Michael Thomas Streeter　　　　　　　　Other
Lift Bridge In Burlington, Ontario

Jolly Sarkar　　　　　　　　Nature
It's Beautiful

Susan McGrath Vafiadis   Nature
Water Splash In Greece

Everett I. Whitney   Animals/Pets
Mama, What Big Teeth You Have!

Kelly Marie Atherton   Nature
Spring Arrives!

Laura A. Torres   Animals/Pets
Take The Darn Picture

Teresa Graham   Children
Daddy's Girl

Janet Lee Martin   Animals/Pets
Majestic Beast

Sarah Elizabeth Lindner
Other
Results Of Dedication

James T. O'Hagan
Nature
Winter Begins

Helene B. Greenstein
Travel
Belize Harbor

Jill M. May
Animals/Pets
Handsun

Tracy Espinosa
Nature
Winter Stream

Caterina Piga
Animals/Pets
Squirrel On The Tree

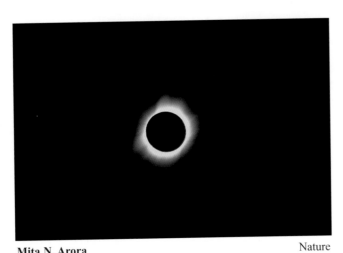

Mita N. Arora   Nature
Total Solar Eclipse — Ghana, March 2006

Preston J. Keable   Nature
Windswept Sunset

Brittany Loren Sicard   Travel
Liberty Light

Nicole J. Perry   Animals/Pets
My Easter Kitties

Terry E. Barton   Animals/Pets
A 'Bird' In A Bath

Jodi Zimmer   Portraiture
Under

Kyle Bradley Minton Nature
Sunset Over Knightdale

Penny Nicole Relaford Nature
Hidden Paradise

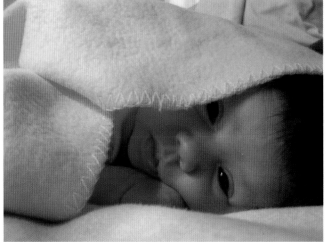

Justin Beaulieu People
My Little Angel

Anna Cranmer Children
My Shadow, My Granddaughter

Linda C. Ferrell Nature
Winter Wonderland

Trevor Isabel Other
Golden Night

Julie Simily Children
Reflections

Erica June Degni Travel
Hawaiian Sunset

Patricia Lupoli Animals/Pets
Snowy Swan

Adam J. Cole Travel
Morning Bridges

Suzanne Elizabeth Moore Nature
Early Morning Rose

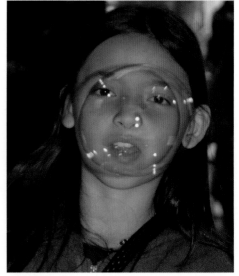

RaeLeene Isabel Adams Children
Bubble Girl

Arnold Domingo Bali Travel
The Many Splendors Of The Rhein

Carol Helmholz Animals/Pets
Deer In Backyard

Cheryl Jade Wildeman Animals/Pets
All Dressed Up And No Place To Go

Frank Steele Smith Children
A Mother's Love

Tal Nissenson Nature
Ice

Ron Lee Snipp Animals/Pets
Red-Tailed Hawk

Catherine Puleo   Children
An Angel Is Born

Michelle Beauchamp   Travel
My Life In Angkor

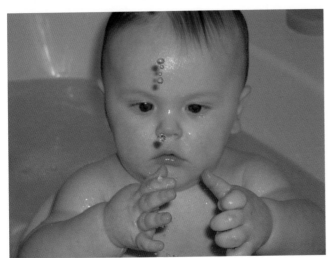

Karen Richardson   Children
Can't Catch Me!

Kirby Wooton   Animals/Pets
Who, Me?

Kristen Marie Trudeau   Animals/Pets
Hummingbird

Angela Campise   Nature
Spring In Texas

Roger Lee Case Children
Football Boo-Boo

Katie Dahl People
Self-Portrait

Kendra A. Timko-Hochkeppel People
Oh, I'm Stuffed!

Lauri Anna Berger Travel
Gateway Arch In Bloom

Aimee Mohr Nature
Pink In Bloom

Joanna S. Hugues Animals/Pets
Ranch Hands

Melissa Jo Wick   Children
Hope

Abigail Claire Watkins   Travel
Reflection Of Amsterdam

Hope Dague   Nature
Morning Dew On A Rose

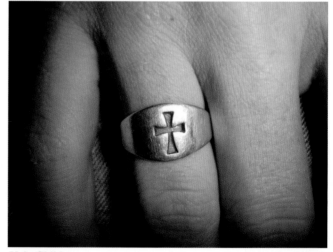

Kyle Childress   Portraiture
Cross Ring

Kathie E. Fitzpatrick   Animals/Pets
Live Monarch Butterfly On Tip Of Finger

Terri L. Kelly   Animals/Pets
Natural Habitat

Tracy Michelle Coy   Children
Twin Love

Christiane Nicole Melroy   Nature
Prayer Time

Amie Mossberger   Nature
Twilight's Peace

Kimberlee Renee Raymond   Children
My First Sparkler

Ally C. Edmund   Other
Tall Wonders Of Seattle, Washington

Misty Lee Walker   Children
Passed Out

Jason Dyke Other
Tunnel

Wayne Keith Lucas Animals/Pets
Here's Looking At You

Michael Kilayko Travel
Sunset At Turtle Bay, Oahu, Hawaii

Luke Keady Nature
Twilight

Danielle Akridge Nature
Trees

Kristina Lynn Hostig Nature
Winter At Singing Beach

Charlene Suzanne Braden   Children
Olivia Asleep On The Job

Gerald Francis Iball   Nature
Bald Eagle

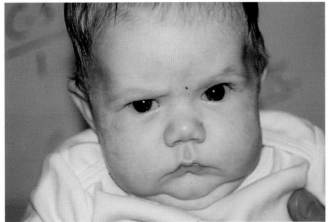

Sue Marie Trudeau   Children
Grumpy Lily

Nikki Roros   Children
Michael's New Sunglasses

Gina Marie Brown   Humor
The Fan

Adam Moreno   Nature
Breaking Through

L. Allan Schaefer   Animals/Pets
Mother And Cub

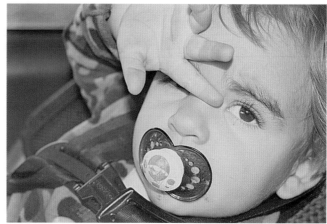

Erika Vieira Matos   Children
Give Me Those Eyes

Sue I. Hylton   Nature
Serenity

Vasiliki Angeline Stavrakis   Nature
Falling In Love In Greece

Ned Allen Kramer   Animals/Pets
True Love

Nancy J. Comparato   Animals/Pets
Hmm, That Sounds Good!

Kevin James Alekna   Nature
Survival Under Extreme Conditions

Jennifer May Armstrong   Children
The Perfect Moment

Naxhieli Acosta   Nature
The Calm Before The Storm

Cameron Bogan Pitman   Nature
Red Hibiscus

Kelsey Thompson   Nature
Cool Trees

Natalie L. Stewart   Nature
African Sunset Reflecting

Shelly LaDon Coleman   Children
Beam Me Up To MeMee And Pop

Rose Marie Cleary   Animals/Pets
Baby Lamb And Mother

Sherry Ann Wilson   Other
Water Beads

Kyla J. Avery   Nature
Serenity

Jerrye Mae Stillman   Animals/Pets
Inquisitive Weasel

Subhra K. Bhattacharya   Travel
Darkness At Noon

Devin Woodworth   Nature
Sunset

Adrienne Kovacs   Nature
Sun Dance

Ted Ornopia Madamba   Children
Sun And Sand

Julie Lucas   Travel
Born To Ride

Amber Hale   Children
Adrianna's First Valentine's Day

Kathleen Marie Visco   Animals/Pets
One, Two, Three, Go!

Thomas Martin Turner Action
Seeing The Elegance

Lorie Jean Shewbridge People
A Family Christmas

Don R. Ishmael People
Look Into My Soul

Debra Eileen Kratz Nature
Grand Canyon

Dora Angelica Torres Children
Torres Tea Party

David Blanc People
Me

Dianna Kay Henshaw   Nature
New Beginnings

Cheryl Borusewicz   Children
Dreams

Ciena Dawn Brodsky   Children
Ciena Dawn At Two Days Old

Noah C. Kirk   Other
Candle In The Dark

Kimberly Anne Skiles   Children
Innocence

Wioletta Kaeseberg   Children
Peek-A-Boo!

Amy E. Brown   Portraiture
Timeless

Nikolas Sebastian Kappy   Other
Lock

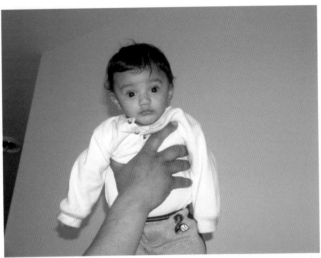

Jessica Roseanna Popolo   People
Mommy's Little Man!

Chelsea Anne Noonan   Animals/Pets
Inquiring Beauty

Polly Wallace   Nature
Mushroom

Laura Ann Daly   Animals/Pets
Fun In The Sun

Richard J. Buza   Animals/Pets
You Talkin' To Me

Dorene K. Goins   Nature
Reflections Of Azalea

Jenna Lynnette Christian   Animals/Pets
My Puppy

Kaitlin Mary Buxell   Nature
Sinking

Bennie F. Reese   Other
Sunset

Tyler Jon Almgren   Nature
Nature Snapshots

Kian Peng Si   Travel
Taronga Zoo, Sydney

James Scott   Other
Untitled

Carolyn J. Miller   Children
Down The Hatch

Susan Broklawski   People
My Pal, Morris

Fumiko Fukuda   Animals/Pets
My Blue Sky

Bonnie Aldrich   Children
My Grandpas Are Vietnam Veterans

Jerry Sawicki Nature
Sunset In Manitoba

Allan Worthington Children
Want A Bite?

Joanne Drake Nature
Bromeliad In Bloom

Pete Barone Travel
What A Party — Route 66

Joan Eisenbeis Children
Trick Or Treat

James Pirtle Children
Rainy Day In Thanlyn

165

Frank W. Wrinn Jr.   Children
Belive This: I Am The American Boy

Allison Chinchilla   Children
Cutie

Julie Naimi   Animals/Pets
Marissa And Her Mystical Cat

Brent Daniel Flynn   Nature
View From Table Mountain

Rose Moe   Animals/Pets
Booth And Friends

Matt George Woodley   Animals/Pets
What Beer You Got In The Fridge, Bro?

Trisha Young   People
Stay Out Of The Water!

Aaron Stroman   Other
Picture Of A Picture

Scout DeWitt   Nature
Reflections Of An April Afternoon

Connie Lynn Rodriguez   Travel
Vesuvius

Robert Dean Harrington   Nature
Incoming Storm

Theresa Marie Norsworthy   Children
Simple Pleasures

Brian J. Bush   Nature
Running Water

Julie Diane Caris   Children
Daddy's Little Man

Heidi M. Bourrie   Nature
Smoky Horizon

Ann Marie Smith   Children
Autumn Wonder

Doris J. Fontaine Casey   Animals/Pets
Colorado Bobcat

Cindy L. Lesky   Nature
Family Time

Glen F. Hudson   Nature
Cherry Blossoms

Scott D. Ferguson   Children
Her First Ocean Sunset

Kimberly Jo Harrison   Nature
Arizona's Setting Sun

Elena Alvarez   Children
Happiness

Kristina Johnson   People
Bittersweet

Dana Errol Wright   People
Cowboy Life

Annette Foshee   Nature
Fishing

Rob W. Kennedy   Nature
Petaluma River

Marla Kane   Animals/Pets
If You Must Work, I Must Nap!

Fred Jafarzadeh   People
Modeling

Elke Houghton   Travel
Sunset Magic

Trisha R. Hogan   Nature
Gull On The Wind

Sonya Landers　　　　　　　　　　　　　　Nature
Spring

Joshua Jay Morlan　　　　　　　　　　　　Children
Can't Always Get Our Way

Chelsea Pfeiffer　　　　　　　　　　Animals/Pets
Kolohe 'Oli

Kathryn Bowen　　　　　　　　　　　　Children
Simple Delight

Kim Massie　　　　　　　　　　　　　　Children
Chocolate Bliss

Alan Francis Gwizdowski　　　　　　　　Nature
Countryside Sunset

Kristin Bierbaum Nature
Mirror Coast

J.D. Sicke Animals/Pets
Huntin' Buddies On Break

Christine Dorothy Horrell Nature
Gerringong, New South Wales

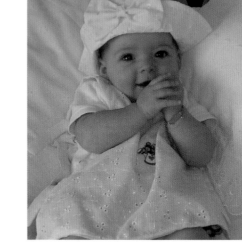

Elaine Fay Gowling Children
Chloe

Marcus Allen Awbrey Nature
Sunflower Rainbow

Danny L. Sugden Nature
Easter Tulip

Jarek Blaminsky
Animals/Pets
Rivals

Sue Kathleen Dobson
Animals/Pets
Zoe, The Jack Russell Pup

Jack Herrera
Animals/Pets
Spurs Jack

Kelly M. Dowdy
Children
Hi, Nana

Raymond M. Porelle
Nature
River Bend

Sharon Ann Rosati
Animals/Pets
Freedom

Kayla Lundeen Animals/Pets
Sleeping Puppy

Todd Anthony Carusi Travel
Old Mining Building

Dick Winters Other
London Bridge

Mary Hall Travel
Sorrento Sunset

Stan Brewer Nature
Mt. Moran Glacier

Charlotte Angela Belicek Children
Innocence

Bridgett Pauline Lamb
Grazing Time

Animals/Pets

Alec B. Weisman
The Perfect Swan

Animals/Pets

Karen Jennifer Knutt
Mommy's Sweet Boy

Children

Karen Edith Hagemeister
Ray Of Sunshine

Nature

Marisa Maney
Best Friends

Children

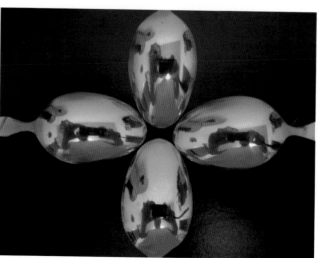

Nick D. Cirillo
Spoonman

Other

Dee Murray Brister   Animals/Pets
Sunday Afternoon

Christopher Isaac McCarthy   Children
A Day At The Beach

Donna Jeanne Perry   Children
Queen Of Hearts

Hannah Jean Argue   Travel
Stormy Seas — St. Lucia, West Indies

Marla Marie Perrin   Nature
Under The Pine Needles

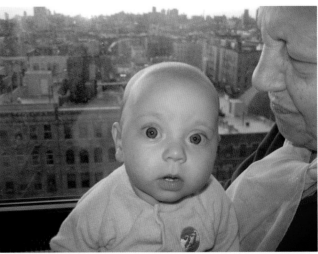

Sabella Monin Rodriguez   Children
A View From Above

Rachel Peralta   Animals/Pets
Akeela

Kristina Jean Howells   Nature
A Snowy Day

Marcy Lynn Jenkins   Nature
Loons On The Lake

Michael Raymond Cayen   Portraiture
A Moment Frozen In Time

Melissa Tyler   Children
Tulip Peek-A-Boo

Alex Filip   Sports
Go Wild

John P. Baniqued   Travel
St. Stephen's Cathedral, Gyor, Hungary

Sowmya Krishnamurthy Siri   Nature
Magical Feeling

Nathan Andrew Sickmiller   Children
One Thousand Words

Deb Kruse   Children
Bad Hair Day!

Jacqui S. Graham   Nature
Secret In The City

Teresa A. Amberg   Children
Messy Ian

Amber Leigh Camp
Roy Boy   Children

Larry Darnell
Christmas Card   People

Tiffany Jane Daniels
Beautiful Baby Girl   People

Mekemeke Ha'unga
Vava'u Sunset   Travel

Johanna Lindsay Murrell
Time Out   Children

Catherine Anne Howatson
Iceland   Nature

Hoi Shan Wong
Children
Fun At The Beach

Huong Vo
Nature
Simple Things

Eileen M. Pellegrini
Children
What Are You Thinking?

Joe Andrew Engle III
Animals/Pets
Come Closer

Tammy Lynne Garland
Children
Inquiring Minds

Adette Deering
Other
Long Jetty

Katrina Maree Woods   Nature
Life At Its Best

Courtney Stuck   People
Boo On Bridge

Charlene Claire Summers   Children
Spaghetti Time

Jason Grischkat   Nature
Mossy Creek

Kimberley Anne Dye   Nature
Alaskan Glacier

Nancy Jordan Cooper   Children
Riley's First Kiss

Jeanette Yvonne Wilson
Nature
Sunset

Michelle Mickelson
Travel
Split Rock Lighthouse

Rafeal Dermundo Graves
Animals/Pets
Monkey Around

Dorothy Dianne Wilcox
Other
Past Repairs

Andrew Lubke
Children
Kevin At Two Years Old

Janine Ruth Heaton
Animals/Pets
Bath Time

Kerry Gail McLoughlin Travel
Sunset In Krabi, Thailand

Marjorie Allan Animals/Pets
My Baby

Taylor Ryann Wessling Nature
Prosperity Of A Leaf

Sheryl Ann Andrews Nature
Beauty And The Bee

Kathryn Elizabeth Grace Smith Animals/Pets
Bad Hair Day (I'm Not Getting Up)

Sharon E. Barber Animals/Pets
Wrestling Budgie

Candice Hobdy   Nature
Peaceful

Brittany Ray Walsh   Nature
Every Petal Fell Off Again

Karel J. Fordyce   Animals/Pets
Can It Be Fixed?

James Lackie   Action
Missed

Abby Corrina Homer   Children
A Special Moment

Raeleen Rose Harwin   Nature
My Red Night

Don Durr   Humor
College Life

Alfonso Campa   Children
Waves And Waves And Waves

Elsie Wood   Animals/Pets
Best Friends

Kerry Dodds   Nature
Autumn Jewels

Isabel Anne McLaren   Children
Best Buddies

David Butler   Other
Big Face

Hal Alexander Butterfield   Animals/Pets
Christmas Puppy

Sarah Kennedy   Nature
Thailand

Bob McAndrews   Nature
Moses Lake Sunrise

Kerry Owen Thomson   Animals/Pets
Hangin' Out

Cachel Childress   Animals/Pets
Lightning

Kristina Lois McGuiness-King   Animals/Pets
Jungle Exploration

Julie Mae Brusselback
Ryan And Friends
Children

Bryan Haven Austin
Spring
Children

Dene Marie Hopkins
King Valley Sunset
Nature

Hilda Conklin
My Cutie Pie
Children

Joanelle Cabrera
In Style
Children

Steven C. Hughes
Gone Fishing
Children

Tara L. Juresh
Sports
No Limits

Gina M. Zompanis
Nature
June Beauty

Maggie Wong
Children
Innocence

Greg Thomas
Nature
Flowers At Sunset

Andrea Danielle Hayes
People
Sisters

Carol Jean Neumann
Children
Already Sees The Beauty Of Life

Michele E. Raffel   Children
Madison

Elizabeth Robyn Jansen   Animals/Pets
Sherman's Boot

Teri Lynne Layman   Nature
Waterfall Miracle

Jorj Niemi   Nature
Bridge At Stow Lake

Dawn B. Giannini   Children
Thoughtful Marie

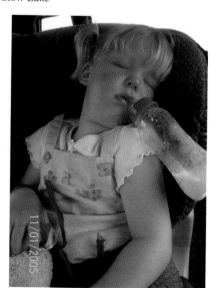

Karen E. Russell   Children
Zzz

Alanna Moldenhauer
Turtle Rock

Nature

Michelle Lynne Gross
The Love Of My Life

People

Kelsey Swenson Grubb
In Flight

Other

Jill Link
Bear

Animals/Pets

Jessica Lynn Comeaux
Tender Memories

Children

Rowan Romeyn
A Long Road Traveled

Portraiture

Roxanna Alejandra Abrines   Nature
Light Breached Through The Clouds

Karl Wagner   Nature
Butterfly

Jordan Reece   Other
Spring Forest

Corneilius Mitchell Brown   Animals/Pets
Stalker

Elizabeth Davey   Animals/Pets
Slip, Slop, Slap

Jane Dimler   Children
Look, Mom, I'm Dancing

Sonya Montana O'Shields   Children
Instance Love

Kimberly A. Ulm   People
Butterfly

Clifford Brown   Children
My First Grandson

Craig S. Koteles   Nature
Tranquil Falls

Angela T. Frizalone   Nature
Day's Deserved Dusk

Kelsey Schnaitman   Other
Wine Glass

Rachel L. Tegyi
Mya On Bike

People

Cindy S. Harms
Audrey

Children

Mellissa D. Nichols
In Flight

Nature

Kristie Lynn Gartner
Is This My New Puppy?

Other

John Gordon May
Gills And Glitter

Travel

Elia E. Acevedo
Josh And Muffin

Animals/Pets

Enid Gaddy
Cracking Up

Children

Robert W. Miller
Untitled

Nature

Lisa Alent
Number One Michigan Wolverine Fan

Children

Robert Joseph Conti
Where The Buffalo Roam

Nature

Linda Lee Scyoc
One In The Tree

Animals/Pets

Jessica Weight
The Grin

Animals/Pets

Joyce L. Brackett   Animals/Pets
Rough Life

James D. Bokus   Nature
My Backyard

Dixie L. Tibbetts   Nature
The Small Gifts

Mia S. Stuesser   Travel
Rick's Cafe, Negril, Jamaica

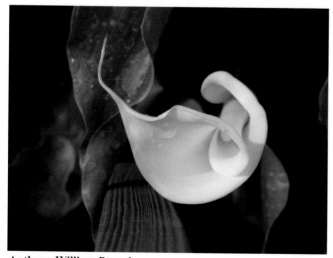

Anthony William Purnel   Nature
Day After The Storm

Kari Lee Schmidt   Other
Sony

Allison Katen
Nature
Pinot Noir

William Kalyna
Travel
Aruba Sunset

Jean Marie Sarchet
Children
Thoughts

Jason Dirks
Nature
Olympic Sunset

Michael Paul Shaw
People
Intriguing

Le Nguyen
Children
Ty's First Easter

Jessica Pierce Herbert   Children
Innocence

Helen Marie Hill   Nature
Zimmerman's Rose

Kate Messersmith   Children
Little Girl

Sarah Louise Hofacker   Children
Spring In Bloom

Teressa Ann Hatley   Animals/Pets
Puppy And Baby Love

Marissa Leanne Fortmuller   People
Air Force Brother

Rebecca A. White
The Joy Of Spring

Nature

Karen Eileen Vanderhaar
Knight's Point, New Zealand

Travel

Allister John Loughran
Mirrored Outback

Other

Tayler Humes Sansbury
Imagine

Portraiture

Audra J. Perry
In The Valley

Nature

Christopher and Kimberly Mayfield
Jaydin

Children

Cindy E. Storie   Nature
Tranquil Moments

Michelle Emily Wayne   People
Smelling The Flower

Ben James   Animals/Pets
Nap Time

Tracy Gail Hudson   Animals/Pets
On The River Thames

Barbara Skocz   Animals/Pets
Bad Day At The Beach

Barbara Gardzina   Nature
Mirror

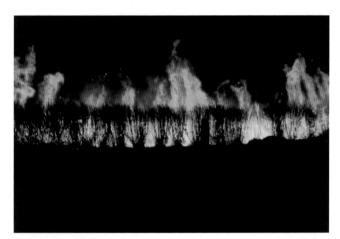

Rae Joanne Haakmeester   Other
Sugar Cane Burn

Christine Sherrer   Animals/Pets
Rachael's First Christmas

Jake Petkau   Animals/Pets
Free Ride

David Thomas Pennal   Travel
Italy

Laura Ann Brown   Animals/Pets
Easter Egg Hunt (I Found One!)

Timothy James Lawrence   Travel
Nice, France

Christina Blacketer — Nature
Torrance Beach

Nettie C. Harris — Nature
A River's Life

Douglas H. MacLachlan — People
Memories

Kenneth James Billington — Other
Oldsmobile

Anna Inthara — Travel
Human-Nature Alliance

Eric Thomas Curran — People
My Little One

Becky Ann Greensage Children
Beach Boy

Glenn R. McColl Animals/Pets
The Bears Of Bern

Jenna Christina Rehnborg Sports
Trailing

Melissa Titus Thomas Children
The Joy Of A Grandchild

Shauna M. Anderson Animals/Pets
Tobi And Nila

Shelly A. Barnes Other
A Lonely Street Lamp

Larry J. Boucher
Nature
Nature's Reflection

Kristy Lee
Children
Beauty

Kali Alfaro
People
Homeless

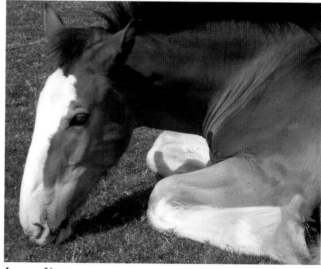

Lorena Young
Animals/Pets
Nature

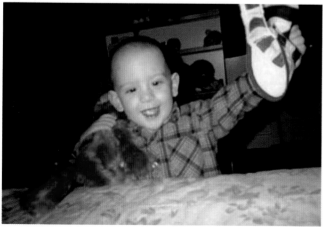

Jane Marie Mangum
Children
Child's Hello

Nicole Marie Berti
Other
Martinis

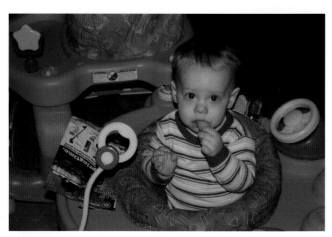

Luke Douglas Carter   Children
Luke

Barbara Ebeling   Portraiture
Chelsea's Second Christmas

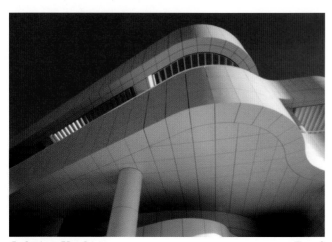

Judy Ann Ketchum   Travel
The Getty

Jennie Marie Ramirez   Animals/Pets
Like Mother, Like Daughter

Melanie Marie Hollingsworth   Animals/Pets
Morning Light

Hugo J. Chavez-Rey   Animals/Pets
Max's Hard Work In The Snow

Dale B. Hardin   Other
Nails For Breakfast

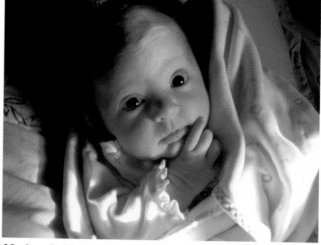

Marlena D. Morrell   Children
Jade Alize'

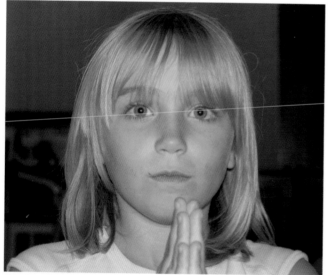

Linda Kay McClung   Children
Child Praying

Derek Cantrell   Portraiture
Chelsea

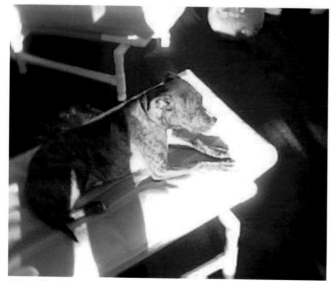

Mike Hewett   Animals/Pets
My Pit Bull

Jaclyn Aileen Hunter   Children
So Simple, Such Pure Beauty

Rachel L. Garfi
Divine Equine
Animals/Pets

Jung Un Hoi
Between Winter And Spring
Portraiture

Stephanie Joyce Davis
Sugar Baby
Animals/Pets

Amanda Marie Rosinski
Illumination
Other

Rodney A. Halbleib
Motherly Love
Animals/Pets

Patrick Venner
Family At The Ocean
People

Lynda S. Davis
Where To, Dad?

Children

Autumn Marie Pregizer
Sunny Day

Other

Monty A. Godsey
Sunset Dragon

Nature

Bryan Davidson Sproles
Israeli Flag At Auschwitz Crematorium Ruins

Other

Gayla Lynn Coppler
Outback Trail

Nature

Sofiya Mateshko
Spring Bloom

People

David H. Lewis   Animals/Pets
Boy Catches Frog

Candace LaCombe   Humor
Thank You, Santa!

Marjorie Katherine Milano   Nature
Tandem Flying

Erik Voake   Children
Iraqi Girls

Jim Minton   Animals/Pets
Friends

Haylee Snyder   Nature
Nature

Oksana Antonova
Friends?

Animals/Pets

Candy Grace Hunter
Mom's Wonders

Nature

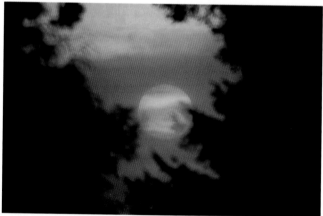

Linda Charles
Idaho Sunset

Nature

Juliana S. Diaz
Awe Inspired

Nature

Jamie D. Town
On The Lake

Children

Angelo J. Sandoval
Careta Vieja En Valle De Allende

Travel

Kent Dickens   Animals/Pets
Spring Fawn

Robyn Nugent Frame   Children
Precious Boy

Debbie Daly   Children
Innocence

Brandi Rae Kaup   People
Proud American

Stan Lemmon   Nature
Tranquility

R. Elaine Lake   Nature
Waterfalls

Vera Collier Animals/Pets

Draped Kitten

Alia Dawn Ferguson Animals/Pets

Sleeping Sisters

Douglas Carl Arnold Nature

African Gold

Joshua Ray Paul Children

Early Learning

Winnie Elizabeth Moncrief Children

In Daddy's Boots

Jennifer Nebert People

Lost Love

John Dunthorne Travel
Mallorca

Julie Cristine Lozano People
Cousins

Irene Olivares People
Troop 630

Rebecca Ruth Baker Children
Son

Jennifer D. Ruth Children
Sisters

Toni Burrough Nature
Somebody Bigger Than You And I

Paige Marie Schartz Travel
Serenity At Sea

Dawn Jeffers Nature
After The Rain

Colleen Melisz Humor
Ethan

Stephanie Kay Eyles People
Fiji Shopkeepers

Leah Nicole Black Nature
At The Beach

Shannon Marie Bish Other
Chrome

Marlene M. Rugg Children
Frankenstein's First Halloween

Barbara Jeanne Burgess Animals/Pets
Where's Lunch

William John Marchioni Children
Jamie Lee

Debbie Goodenough Other
Sacrifice

Rachael Leigh Wright Nature
Endless

David Benardout Animals/Pets
Bliss

Niki Gai Albury   Sports
Jolby

Tina Stivers   People
Youngest Cheerleader!

April Willsey   Nature
The Old Mill

Caesar W. Desiato   Animals/Pets
The Queen At Christmas

Craig Stuart Davidson   Nature
Mississippi Gorge

Julie Ann Ogles   People
Rose On St. Patrick's Day

Shannon Della Hunt   Nature
Country Scenery

David Estelle Gwaltney   Humor
Handicapped?

Lisa Marie Hebert   Children
Beautiful Baby

Roland G. Murphy   Nature
Nature Walk

Beth Laws Gragg   Children
Serenity By The Sea

Carmela Berdan   Children
I'm Done Trick-Or-Treating

216

Marion Groetzmeier Algier   Animals/Pets
Beach Friends

Mary Anna Arnott   Children
Fishing At Pond Meadow Park

Lana Highfill   Animals/Pets
Morpheus

Jeffrey Caporaso   Nature
Amber Sky

Barbara Yvonne VerHaar   Animals/Pets
New Buddies

Brenda E. Birk   Nature
Tulip

Amber Jolly   Animals/Pets
Jayce And His Puppies

Brandi Hill   Nature
Untitled

Jana Smith   Children
I Want To Be In Pictures

ARTISTS' PROFILES

ABELING, PAM B.
Candid photos are my favorite and my two grand-children, Kasey and Adian, are my favorite subjects. We go to this playground quite often and on this day, Kasey decided this lion needed to be quiet. I'm thrilled that I caught this sweet, spontaneous moment. I wait patiently to capture scenes like this. I love to share photos with my friends and family, especially those who live far away. They get to see Kasey and Adian as they grow up and I get to show off my photography I am always working on!

ALGIER, MARION GROETZMEIER
I have loved photography all my life! I always have a camera with me. "Beach Friends" was taken on New Year's Day in Laguna Beach, California. My husband, Tim, and I were contemplating the upcoming year with our Chihuahua, Angel. It was a perfect moment on a perfect New Year's Day. My passion, besides photography, is writing and I hope someday to combine the two.

ALMGREN, TYLER JON
This is a photo of a vinca vine flower. I live in Massachusetts and took this picture in my cousin's backyard in April. I am twelve years old and love taking pictures, so I decided to send one of them in. It's not the best one, but it is one of my favorites. This picture will be preserved forever.

ALWARDT, CHRISTOPHER
Being a lover of myths and history, this photo reminded me of the great travelers of the Old World: Jason, Sinbad, and the other "gods" of old.

AMERENA, BILL
The picture "My Pal" is of my cat, Bucky, with his paw around his mother, Fluffy. Fluffy was a stray cat that had four kittens outside of my house. I found them and decided to keep them all. They are always together. I was able to take photos and video of the kittens growing up with their mother.

ANDREWS, CHRIS
This is a photo taken from a street in New York City. I was on my way home from the Comic-Con, a comic convention, and was taking some pictures with my digital camera. This was my favorite one of the bunch. I like the way the buildings look against the cloudy blue sky.

ANDREWS, SHERYL ANN
I have always been interested in photography. Now that I have a digital camera, I am having much more success. I can click away to my heart's content and once the photos are loaded onto the computer, I can check them out and print the special ones. I still have a lot to learn and have been attending photography classes. We have some magnificent scenery here in New Zealand — a great place to explore and photograph. I also appreciate the beauty of roses and have a number of these iceberg roses growing in my garden.

ARELLANO, RICK
I have always been interested in photography, but I never took it seriously. This is the first photo I have submitted for a contest. About a year ago, I bought myself a decent camera and I have been

impressed with some of my photos. "Heavenly Shine" was a photo I took on the beach of Cozumel, Mexico. I experienced this trip with a group of wonderful people I work with in Portland, Oregon. I was so amazed with this photo that I felt I had to share it with the world.

ARGUE, HANNAH JEAN
This photo was taken on a Windjammer cruise through the West Indies. I was lying on my bunk looking out the porthole. It was the first of two pictures taken. Growing up canoeing and camping, I developed a great appreciation of the outdoors, nature, and a love to travel. I always have my camera with me for those unexpected moments I want to save forever. I photograph my travels in order to share with others the beautiful places that I have visited. I feel so honored to have been selected for publishing, considering this was my first submission made toward my pursuit of some type of career in photography.

ARTER, COREY SCOTT
As a communication artist, I am continuously seeking moments that convey a vivid sense of emotion and introspection. In the case of this particular photographic opportunity, I happened to be strolling along the Mississippi River with my sister. She sat down on the remains of a tree and looked out onto the river as tears welled up in her eyes. I saw this moment as one of truth — an image that conveys the uncertainty and possibility life has to offer.

ATHERTON, ANTONIA V.
I saw this squirrel with his tail fluffed out; clearly he was agitated about something. I took a distant shot and was puzzled to see black and white stripes in the photo. I realized it was a rattlesnake that had the squirrel so excited. I very cautiously got closer and snapped this picture. The snake had nine rattles and was one of the biggest I've ever seen. The snake then made a U-turn and slithered into a hole. I'm a registered nurse and my husband is a retired police detective, and we love to ride and show horses.

AVERY, KYLA J.
I enjoy taking pictures of everyday life. I've been taking pictures for about one year and nature photos are definitely my favorite. I came across this photo when I was out on a walk; I had my camera just in case something caught my eye. I'm a big fan of covered bridges, so I went camera crazy. "Serenity" is my favorite picture of the bunch. There is just something about the photo that captured a special place in time.

BACZEK, JEANNIE MARIE
Photography has been a hobby of mine since I was a child. "First Snow" is a photo of my dogs at seven months old; they were amazed at the cold, white flakes falling to the ground and had to investigate. The look on their faces was priceless. This shot allowed me to capture this moment forever. I'm a big outdoors and animal fan, so when I have the chance to document nature and its beauty, I don't hesitate to take out my camera. I'm honored to be able to share my photos with other individuals that enjoy the same medium.

BALDWIN, MARIE T.
Being raised as a traditional Native American taught me to see beauty in everything around me, including the flowers blooming in my own front yard. When I took this photograph, I was actually practicing with a new camera. The colors I saw through the lens were so lovely, I just snapped off several shots, and this was one of them. I never thought it would be published!

BALI, ARNOLD DOMINGO
While in Germany on business, I was in the market for a digital camera. After purchasing one, I had the weekends to venture out and explore Europe. I visited Austria, Switzerland, France, and the Netherlands. Europe is so amazing with its breathtaking scenery, "postcard towns," great food, and friendly people. The shot I took on the Rhein River is my favorite. It depicts the castle that has stood there for hundreds of years, the Rhein itself, and the famous vineyards. I hope you'll enjoy this picture as much as I do!

BARONE, PETE
This is a scene along Route 66 in California where our family was vacationing. This scene captured my interest and I wanted to preserve it in memory through a picture. My family consists of my wife, Debra, and my two sons: Stefan and Jordan. I am a communications project manager in New York City and I have a master's degree in project management. My interests are photography, music, and travel, to name a few. Enjoy life!

BASKIN, LOUIS MICHAEL
My back porch is a favorite dining place for all the creatures that live in the woods behind my house. This chipmunk was the first visitor of its kind. He obviously arrived before I had a chance to refill the dish. He's been back many times since.

BEASLEY, DAWN M.
We went to Lake Martin for our anniversary. There is a nesting area there with thousands of birds. I was taking pictures of them when my husband tapped my shoulder and told me to look down with my camera. Sure enough, about thirty feet away from me was an alligator. We went around the lake to the marshy area. Across a slough, there was a patch of land and that is where we found him. He was watching some kids along our side of the slough. I decided to name the alligator "Herman."

BECKER, ROSE V.
I stumbled into photography by accident. Approximately two years ago, I attended a circus in Rutherford, New Jersey, and brought my camera along. After having my pictures developed, I was quite amazed with the ones I took of the trapeze act — acrobats fly through the air. I took a photography class at a community college located in my area and learned the basics of photography. I am a true Aquarius and love the water. When I was visiting Baltimore, Maryland, I wanted to tour the aquarium. While walking through the exhibits, I noticed the divers preparing to go into the tank. The diver who is in the picture waved to me while I was outside of the tank.

BECKWITH, CANDACE MELANIE
My love for photography has grown with time. I

enjoy photographing people and capturing their emotions, their cultures, religion, color, etc. They all make good subjects for me and they all have a great story to tell.

BEDDOWS, SUSAN L.
I love all types of pictures, and taking them as well. While at a family gathering, we were all sitting around a large fire chatting and having a great time. I was taking pictures of everyone and decided to take a picture of the flames in front of me. Most times people think of fire and they link it to destruction, but this picture is different. This photo captured the beauty within fire, the beauty that makes fire hypnotic.

BELICEK, CHARLOTTE ANGELA
This photo was taken Easter Sunday 2006. The girls in the photo (right to left) are Paige and Hannah, two of my nieces, and the third girl is my cousin's granddaughter, Carrie. The trio was very busy chasing large bubbles produced by Hannah's older brother, Spencer.

BERMUDEZ, JUAN CARLO
This is a photo I took in December 2006 in Quimbaya. It is a small village in the mountains of Columbia, South America. This area is extremely Catholic, but they also have a strong respect for the gods of the pre-Columbian cultures. This child was in charge of the candles for the fire ritual. Next year, they will start to decorate the candleholders. This celebration is held every December.

BERTI, NICOLE MARIE
Photography has always been a hobby of mine, so I was thrilled to receive a professional camera as a high school graduation present from my parents. In college, I took a photography class that had an assignment using depth of field. I thought that the use of martini glasses would really be interesting. Only being able to see the one full glass in this picture, I believe, gives it a better perspective and meaning. So thanks for the camera, Mom and Dad, it really works!

BIRK, BRENDA E.
This tulip was in the flowerbed in my front lawn — it was the only one this color. If you believe in fairies, there is one in this picture. She is picking dandelions in the upper left corner! If you don't believe in them, then it's just a leaf!

BLOSSER, MARY KAY
I've visited the ocean often, but have never had the energy to rise early enough to see the sunrise. Recently we visited friends at Myrtle Beach, South Carolina, and my friend, Jack, asked me to do just that. With a cup of coffee in hand, he and I headed out to the beach at five the following morning. We sat in the van, waiting for the day to unfold — the wait was worth it. Little by little, the Lord unveiled His beauty around us. This was one of many beautiful pictures we captured on film.

BOLLIN, DIXIE FAE
I am a factory worker with twenty-five grandchildren. I do not consider myself a photographer at all. Since our children have gone from home, my husband and I have fallen in love with English

mastiffs. This is our fourteen-month-old "son," Duke, named after John Wayne. He is one of eighteen mastiff children we own.

BORUSEWICZ, CHERYL
This is a picture of my daughters, taken at Disney World at sunrise. I took the picture in hopes that it would capture the innocent, unlimited possibilities the future can hold for them, as long as they hold onto their dreams. I was surprised of the outcome and how pure the picture came out. The original is in color and captures every bit of light that makes this picture priceless to me. I submitted the black and white to show the dramatic effect. I wanted them to look at this picture together and remember to always dream.

BOSLEY, HUNTER
After my last year of high school, I had the opportunity to spend several months in British Columbia, Canada. I lived on a fishing resort as a maintenance worker, spending my daylight hours traveling to and from this tiny island. Nearly everywhere you looked, an award-winning photograph could have been taken. One particular view stood out during my days living there, where a tall steel fish smoker stood alone in the forest. Like the smoker, I realized that I too was isolated from the outside world, but stood tall and revealed myself to what was there.

BOUNDY, CRAIG JOHN
I went camping at Cedar Grove in Queensland, Australia, and borrowed my friend's little camera. On the first morning of camping, I woke extra early, grabbed the camera and headed off through the bush. I have never done anything with photography before, but I soon realized the scenes I captured are the ones that told me to take them! I feel like nature is a beautiful lady and at certain times, if you have the eye to notice her, she poses for you — all you have to do is ask her to smile.

BOUTHILLIER, MONIQUE MARIE
This picture captures one of the few quiet moments with my daughter, Kaelyn; she was one month old at the time. Needing her mother's love to help her feel better, rocking her to sleep was the only way to get some rest after a whole night of her crying. She kept me up until five in the morning!

BOWEN, KATHRYN
After a long day at Disneyland, my nephew, my sister, and I got ice cream cones to cool down. We sat on the sidewalk of Main Street, waiting for the evening parade to begin. This was the most relaxing part of the day for all of us.

BOWMAN, COURTNEY
I took this picture during my last year of college. My father, an artist and an inspiration, took pictures that captured a mood with shadow and light. This photograph shows the influence of graphic design, the field I would soon enter, emerging in my work. "Stairs" also reminds me of why I love photography: the artist can take an everyday object or scene, in its truest form, and depict that image in an unexpected perspective.

BOYER, KIMBERLY DAWN
Mallory is our first grandchild. She has been such

a wonderful experience! We are so fortunate to be included in every aspect of her arriving. I'll never forget her tiny beautiful face as she pushed her way into our world and my heart. She is such a sweet, free-spirited little girl and she has forever changed our lives. Because of her presence, I want to be a better person. As I took this photo, I imagined her as "our little angel fairy." Our whole family loves her so very much; she is truly a blessing.

BRANT, DONNITTA K.
This is a picture of my granddaughter at two days old. Her parents did all that they could to conceive. They lost the twin eight weeks into the pregnancy and then my granddaughter was born two months premature, weighing only two pounds, two ounces. With God at her side, she fought to stay alive and won. She is nine months old now and doing great!

BRANTLEY, WENDY
"Peek-A-Boo" is a favorite family photograph. It was taken when some dear friends invited us to Paramount's Carowinds, an amusement park in Charlotte, North Carolina. We had just been caught in an unexpected thunderstorm. Our daughter, Christa, two years old, was playing peek-a-boo near a tree. It is a pleasant surprise to learn that this photograph will be published. I have always loved taking pictures; they immortalize our memories. Beauty is all around us, just take out your camera, capture the moment, and share it with the world.

BRENNAN, MARCIA J.
I have always loved this photo of our grandson, Dylan. I believe the look on Dylan's face is priceless. On a whim, I decided to submit it in your photo contest. This is the first photo contest I've ever entered and I was absolutely thrilled to find out that this photo has been selected for publication in your book. This has definitely provided me with the momentum I need to pursue my love of photography. It has also given me the confidence to pursue other photo opportunities as well.

BRISTER, DEE MURRAY
This photo was taken on a Sunday afternoon. I was watching my husband play catch with our collie, Oscar, in the pasture behind our house in Tallahassee, Florida. We often play with Oscar in the pasture, if you look closely at the photo you can see another of his toys stuck in the tree above him. For this photo, Oscar had paused for a bit before running after his Frisbee, just as he stopped I snapped the picture.

BROWN, CLIFFORD
My first grandson, whom I was blessed with from my youngest daughter, a Marine, lives in Japan with his father and her. The photograph was taken on a cruise ship at my oldest daughter's wedding in January 2006. I always have my camera with me; I take pictures of every opportunity I get. When my grandson walked up to me on the cruise ship there it was, the perfect shot.

BROWN, DESIRAE GAYLE
Photography has always been a hobby I enjoy. My husband and I moved to Wyoming for a short time while he worked with a coal company there.

This gave me the opportunity to see a beautiful range of sites, not found in Kentucky. "Afternoon Graze" is a shot I took while on a day trip to Flaming Gorge, located on the Utah-Wyoming border. It was also my husband's favorite picture from our trip. Beauty can be found in anything, so I'm never without my camera. Always remember that beauty is in the eye of the beholder. If something touches you, it's beautiful.

BROWN, LISA MARIE
Shawna Marie passed away on February 24, 2006. She was fifteen years old and an angel sent from Heaven. This picture was one of many that were shared at her funeral services. Shawna was a patient at St. Jude Children's Research Hospital in Memphis, Tennessee, and was loved by many! I hope everyone that sees her photo enjoys it as much as I do! Thank you for letting me share my angel with you all! Her memory will live on forever. She was also wearing her hope necklace from St. Jude — she never took it off.

BROWN, SANDI KAY
A widow of three years, I bought Panzer from a local breeder in Lexington, Kentucky. She is a one-and-a-half-year-old tortoiseshell Persian. She loves wine out of a straw. She is my constant companion; she rides in my boat and with me on my horse. She is a total joy.

BROWN, TAMMY G.
The story behind this photo is special to me. My name is Tammy Brown. My family and I live in Tennessee where we have many tornadoes. I will never forget the sound of my son's voice in a phone conversation we had over two years ago. While escaping a tornado, he watched our house that he just exited disappear. Recently, we heard the news announced that a tornado had been spotted near us. We snapped a few pictures and went inside. We preoccupied everyone by looking through the pictures. That's when we found her just starting to float from behind the clouds, watching over us.

BROWN, WARREN H.
This photo was taken while I was working in northern Quebec, near the James Bay Area. As a field geologist, I have an opportunity to see the splendor and raw beauty of nature. I am glad to share these images with my family and friends, and now with all of you.

BRUNE, OLIVIA MAE
I personally challenge anyone who says pit bulls are mean to stop and take a look at this adorable mug. My boyfriend, Adam, and I are police officers in Jacksonville, Illinois. We encountered Tori on a traffic stop. Adam stopped a vehicle and discovered that the people were transporting drugs. Tori's owners went to jail and she went to the local pound. Knowing what a wonderful dog Tori was, I received permission from her owners and adopted her. Please remember any dog can be mean, it is all in how they are raised.

BURGESS, OPAL TRAJANO
This picture was taken on Valentine's Day when my son, Timothy, was about six months old. He loves playing with small pillows. Timmy is a

happy baby, he doesn't cry or get scared of strangers. He always smiles and is very friendly to everyone. When my husband passed away last April, I moved my family to Texas to start a new life. I also have three other children and they are all great.

BURSTEIN, BRIGITTE L.
Every morning my two-year-old English bulldog, Nuggles, wakes up and can't wait to soak up the sun peering through the window in the living room. As the light shifts, so does Nuggles, crawling and sliding across the floor in search of some much needed sun. Although changing locations several times, Nuggles is careful not to overdo his exercise regime. The lighting and expression on his face told me I had something special that I wanted to keep forever.

BUTLER, DAVID
I love shooting great scenes; I enjoyed shooting this exotic fountain at Millennium Park. Using a wide-angle lens on my camera, it gives the big face a larger perspective with the tall buildings in the background. On the surface, it really looked like hard work in the dark room, but I created this from the digital darkroom. After I get the film developed, I use a good film scanner and digitize the film into the computer. Living in Chicago, I believe it is a beautiful place to visit and Millennium Park is one of its highlights.

BUTTERFIELD, HAL ALEXANDER
Two of my family's three dogs died within months of each other. This left us sad and certain we wouldn't replace them with puppies. Harvey Crumpet was spotted in a pet shop while collecting fish-tank supplies. His cute, wrinkly little face became indelibly stamped in my mind. We returned days later and took him home with us. Our grieving Staffordshire, Jarrah, had been depressed since Harry's death, we all had been to varying degrees. Harvey's character is magnetic and affectionate. In our home, Harvey had a healing effect and is referred to as "Love Doctor."

BUZA, RICHARD J.
Photography has always been my passion. I would like to thank you for helping me feel closer to my dream. I was able to get some of my favorite animal photos at the Utah's Hogle Zoo and spend some time with my girlfriend.

CABRERA, JOANELLE
A new model has taken center stage in the time of high fashion. Her name is Arionne. Her proud daddy, Rynell Calloway, is holding her in this picture. Arionne is modeling the latest fashion on the runway for children. The picture was taken before Ari's first trip to the zoo.

CAMBRIA, SARA
I have this photo hanging in my office. One day, my boss comes in and says, "Your picture is upside down." I kindly told him it was not. He could not understand that every artist sees something different in their work. After a friendly debate, I thought of the perfect name for my photo, "Perspective." The moral of the story is that art and beauty are in the eye of the beholder. Don't ever let anyone tell you that your art is wrong.

CAMMARATA, PETER RALPH
Venice is the most beautiful place I have ever seen. It is filled with so much beauty and history. I feel that "The Gondolier" really captures Venice. I dedicate this picture to my parents and brother, they have always believed in me. I also dedicate this picture to the rest of my family and to the love of my life, Karen.

CAMPISE, ANGELA
This photo was taken in Marble Falls, Texas. It is where my husband and I enjoy going for long weekends, so we can relax and get away from the city. This is just one of the many beautiful scenes to be found there.

CANSLER, NINA L.
This is a photo of a sunrise from the door of my apartment. The hues of the sunrise woke me; they were so incredibly bright. I paint with oils. I will paint this so my family can enjoy it as well.

CARLSON-ACTON, HEATHER EILEEN
This was one of twelve beautiful roses my friend gave me for my thirtieth birthday. She's a wonderful painter, so I originally took this picture for her to paint. But, when I downloaded this photo onto my computer, I was amazed at the detail. So, I promptly printed the photo a few times. I have one framed above my bed, I gave one to my friend for painting, and I have the one you see here. I'm so glad to have this opportunity to share this special rose with you. I hope you enjoy it as much as I do. Thank you.

CARTER, LUKE DOUGLAS
This is a picture of nine-month-old Luke Carter, eating his very first pickle. He loved it!

CASTRO, JOSE RENTERIA
This is a typical photo of my grandson. It seems that he's always happy and so full of life. At three years old, he seems wiser than some adults that I know. My hope is that this photo brings a little of life's cheer into yours. A little smile goes a long way.

CATIZONE, CAROL
I am both an amateur photographer and professional dog trainer that can always be seen with a camera in hand. This photo was taken one afternoon during the last days of winter. It represents how I see nature — simple, but awe inspiring. I am so proud and thankful to be in the company of other amateurs whose photos have been chosen for publication. To be honored in this way has inspired me to follow my dream of becoming a professional photographer.

CAYEN, MICHAEL RAYMOND
One of the most challenging aspects of photography is capturing what our eyes see, especially for an amateur photographer like myself. This photo of my fiancée and her son reflects so many feelings and thoughts, I knew instantly I had stumbled onto one of those rare moments "frozen in time." The title seemed obvious as it was taken inside the famous ice castle at Chateau Lake Louise in Alberta, Canada. I fell in love with this photograph, much like I did with its subject, as soon as I saw it. I hope you enjoy it!

CHANDLER, WILLIAM COLT
This photo was taken during an afternoon walk. I came across a bird feeder in the park and sat on a bench to watch the birds eagerly fight for their spots. It was a lucky snapshot to catch the bird in mid-flight and I was surprised to see the picture turn out as well as it did. I love the fact that I have the power to stop time. As a photographer, you have a time machine in your own hands. I enjoy photography more than any other activity I partake in.

CHANEY, MARY ELIZABETH
I am the youngest member of a Texas family. I recently graduated from Centenary College of Louisiana with a bachelor's degree in communications, with an emphasis in new media. Thanks to my parents, Pam and Dan, I have been able to see and experience so many wonderful aspects in life. Going to college and being able to take a photography class is just one of them. The picture of my family's cat, Tom, was taken while he was asleep. If only life were as simple as a cat's! But since it isn't, there is always room for little cat-naps here and there.

CHANEY, STEPHANIE
I've always had a passion for photography, and the arts. I have a degree in graphic design, but have been more interested in photography since my childhood. I like capturing a variety of subjects: people, flowers, and nature. I'm always looking for that one image that catches my eye and leaves a lasting impression for everyone to see.

CHAVEZ-REY, HUGO J.
This picture was taken during one of Colorado's worst blizzards in history. After being snowbound in our house for four days, we began the task of digging out of about three feet of snow. Max, our West Highland terrier, was very eager to help, as portrayed in the photo. Max loves the snow and had a blast treading through it. West Highlands are a great breed of dog. They are very loyal and feisty, but also very obedient.

CHERNESKY, JAMES WALTER
This picture was taken at Myrtle Beach, South Carolina, between five and six in the morning. There were heavy storms all night. Walking along the overcast beach, there seemingly was no opportunity for beauty. I decided to wait ten more minutes, then daybreak appeared in front of me. Life's greatest opportunities are sometimes so disguised. If we are patient and take the time to look, we can experience the best life has to offer.

CHILDRESS, KYLE
I was in Brisbane, Australia, in May 2006 when I took this picture. I was just trying to figure out how my camera works. I sat on a bench at the bus station and snapped this picture of my hand. It seems to have turned out quite nicely. I love it because it signifies my faith and Jesus is a central part of that faith. I hope that people will look at my pictures and see the purpose and efforts behind all of them. Mostly, I hope that people can see my joy in the artwork.

CHINCHILLA, ALLISON
This photo is of my daughter, Alexia. She is only

four months old in the picture. I love taking photos of my daughter. I often take them every morning when she wakes up because she gives us the most beautiful, natural, innocent expression, almost like an angel. I chose to share this one because the look on her face is so cute! I wanted to keep this memory forever and I am very proud to have captured that.

MAYFIELD, CHRIS AND KIMBERLY
This photo was taken on April 21, 2006 while Jaydin was playing in her swing. Her smile will last a lifetime in our hearts. We love you!

CIRILLO, NICK D.
After growing up around photography, my interests appeared when I got my first digital camera. Fostered by three years of working as a student volunteer zoo guide at the Los Angeles Zoo, my photography has improved tremendously. This stunning photograph was captured at Westlake Village, California, and this was the only time I have ever seen swans there.

CLEARY, ROSE MARIE
I love to take pictures. I never thought that my picture would be in a book. This photo was taken over at my friend's home on a farm. The mother's name is Tootles; she is three years old. She has a twin named Woodles. You can tell them apart by the length of their tales, Tootles' tail is longer. The baby lamb's name is Goofy, and he was born on February 26, 2006.

COLFLESH, TRUDY PATTERSON
My husband, George, and I recently moved from New Jersey to Colorado Springs, Colorado, nestled at the foot of Pikes Peak. We were eager to explore our new area and went hiking often. I wanted to photograph the indescribable beauty around us in some small way or another. While climbing a trail in the foothills of Pikes Peak, we ascended the top of a mound and before us stood an ancient pine. Fluffy clouds in the brilliant sky seemed to arise from the branches of the 2,000-year-old tree, exactly like a burning bush.

COLLINS, FOREST V.
This is a photo of my beautiful daughter and a young deer. I believe that deer are curious by nature. I wish I could capture all of the beautiful moments here in southeast Alaska. These truly are wonderful times.

COMPAGNINO, ANDREA MARY
My husband, Nick, gave me a Canon camera for Christmas about six years ago. I have been shooting ever since! "Yellow Tulips" is one of my favorite pictures. The "reaching out" of the one tulip is symbolic to me; it represents my reaching out to catch the simple beauty that surrounds us every day. That's what I want people to see when they look at this picture, the beauty of nature and a closer, more intimate look into our world. I intend to continue my photography and to improve with every shot.

COMPARATO, NANCY J.
This is a photo of my collie, Sabrina. She is actively out on the show circuit. I was watching the Eukanuba Tournament of Champions Dog

Show when she came in the room and began watching the TV as if she knew what was going on. I tiptoed out to get the camera and when I came back she hadn't moved. When the dog food commercial came on she really perked up, as if to say, "Hmm, that sounds good!" We have three other show collies and they are always keeping us entertained. We have several fun photos of them.

COOPER, NANCY JORDAN
My husband and I work with dolphins. We consider them to be our "kids." Naturally, when our daughter, Riley, was born we had to introduce all of our "kids" to each other. This photo shows our daughter being kissed by our male dolphin, Littlebit. He is a gentle giant whose kiss will make a lasting impression on our little girl.

COPPLER, GAYLA LYNN
I am married to a darling guy currently in the Air Force, and he shares my love of travel. We visited Australia after getting our first digital camera. I rose early one day to catch Uluru (Ayers Rock) at sunrise. The mountain was gorgeous. As I was leaving the lookout hill, something told me to look back. This view was a gift from God.

COY, TRACY MICHELLE
"Twin Love" is a shot I got while babysitting this adorable set of twins. When you take pictures of children in their own environment, it is amazing what they do on their own. I love capturing shots like this; it is one of my personal favorites.

CROOKSTON, JOHANNA MARIA
This photo captured my granddaughter coming from the shower. I think it is a lovely, unexpected photo. She is a two-year-old gem. Georgia lives with her mom, Jo, and dad, Joe, in Galston, a suburb of Sydney, Australia.

CUMMING, DAVE ANDREW
Six friends, and myself, left Torquay, England, on September 10, 2003 for Washington, D.C., and spent the following three weeks traveling across the United States. We stopped at numerous places along the way: Nashville, Memphis, New Orleans, Texas, Arizona, Las Vegas, and finally, Los Angeles. This was one of the many highlights of the trip, taken in late September at the Grand Canyon.

CURRAN, ERIC THOMAS
This is my son, Julian. He was getting ready to go to church when suddenly, he struck some priceless poses. Can't you tell he is such a ham for the camera? He loves smiling at everyone and is sure to be a heartbreaker someday. Watch out ladies!

DAHL, KATIE
This is a picture of me in the early spring. I had been working diligently to keep in shape and this picture commemorates the celebration of hitting my target weight. I was surprised that this photo turned out as well as it did!

DAHM, PETER CHARLES
I captured this image after I just hit my sand wedge and started to climb out of a deep bunker. Turning to look at where my ball landed, this is what I saw. I may have not been the closest to the

pin, but what a view. This was taken on the Seven Canyons Golf Course in Sedona, Arizona. I reached into my bag and pulled out my camera. Just lying on the green gave me a whole new outlook about golf. So now I know, this is "A View From The Green."

DALE, JULIE MAXEY
The security guards parted as I took this photo. I couldn't get the date changed before I took the photo because my time was limited. I knew it was a good shot and so I took it anyway. Pope Benedict leaned forward and shook my hand. At the same time, a professional photographer took a photo of us. This was a special moment in time and your publication keeps it alive in my heart.

DALL, CATHERINE SUSANNE
This photo was taken while my husband and I were kayaking on Margaret River, in Western Australia. We were on our honeymoon, and I was just snapping away, taking dozens of different photos. It wasn't until we had the film developed that I realized what a beautiful shot this was — definitely something to remember from our honeymoon!

DALY, LAURA ANN
I love taking pictures of my animals. Britney is one of my three dogs whom I often take pictures of. Britney hates the water, and especially getting wet. But, when I got my pool and bought her a float, she loved it! I work as a nurse in a nursing home and Britney comes to work with me. She brings smiles and joy to my residents and I hope that this picture will do the same for everyone that sees it.

DANG, CATHERINE
I have been a Disney fan my whole life. I have collected anything and everything that is a keepsake collectible. This is a photo of Penny Lane. I'm surprised she stayed still for the picture. I have my camera with me at all times, so I can capture the memorable moments in life.

DANIELS, TIFFANY JANE
This is a photograph of my seven-month-old daughter, Chasidee. She just barely learned how to hold her head up and smile. She loves to smile at everyone she sees. Her and her brother are so adorable together. They're both old enough to play with each other now, so my son, Dakota, is always running around her dancing and she laughs at him. They are way too cute.

DAVIS, DANIELLE LEE
My husband and I were at Dog Beach in San Diego to watch the sunset. I was just about to snap the picture when this dog walked right in the shot. When I first saw him I almost didn't take it, but I waited. He walked a little further and stopped at the perfect spot.

DE LA CRUZ, JANET
Taking pictures, of trees especially, has been my hobby since I was young. Trees are so free moving, even without a slight breeze. This particular photo was taken while resting along the walkway of flags approaching the famous presidents' faces on Mount Rushmore. As I was standing there, these trees caught my eye. I thought to myself, "I must take this picture!" It was breathtaking and I

hope when others go to Mount Rushmore in South Dakota, they will also notice this section of trees.

DE LEON, JANE
I have recently had the desire to do photography, and I am thrilled that you selected my photo for publication! My boyfriend and I were making a treacherous journey home from Niagara Falls when the picture was taken. We were somewhere along the coast of New York State. There were so many beautiful sights along the way and this was one of them! This photo was taken while we were in motion and I am surprised at how well it came out. Thank you again for picking my photo to be published.

DEBLIECK, TODD
This is a photo I took while serving on a tour in Iraq. I feel that it is a constant reminder of what I've done and seen, as well as what other Marines, sailors, and soldiers are doing on a daily basis, risking their lives for our freedom and the freedom of others.

DEBOER, DUSTIN A.
This was called being in the right spot at the right moment after spending a week of building trail on the North Country Trail! I have always dreamed of being a published photographer and now my company, Solid Rock Photography, is making an impression in the market. I have been published in four different venues, including this publication.

DEJMAL, LYLE DON
I consider every moment of life a still image of time. As one looks at a photo they realize how special that moment was. "Kansas Tree" is an example of seeing one of these special moments. During the twenty-two-mile drive from work in Luray to home in Osborne, I saw this beautiful picture opportunity.

DENTON, JANE EILEEN
I decided to embark on a journey from Arizona to New Brunswick, Canada, with my eight-year-old granddaughter, Veronica, by automobile. We took loads of pictures of the breathtaking scenery during our adventure, and this beautiful lighthouse standing against the Atlantic Ocean was one of them. While the tide was out, I snapped the picture and we watched as the ocean waves surrounded this majestic structure. Being from Arizona, we had never seen anything like this before and probably won't again for sometime! It was a beautiful sight!

DIMLER, JANE
It is sometimes strange how the simple things in life can produce so much joy for those people fortunate enough to find them. This picture exhibits the simple art of expression through dance, but it is the pure joy in my son's face that brings it to life. Sean was fifteen months old when I captured his first attempt at dancing. As many parents can relate, a picture can capture a moment, but there is nothing to the way a child captures a heart.

DIRKS, JASON
This photograph was taken from downtown Seattle, as the sun fell over the Olympic Mountains on a cool spring evening. As an avid outdoor

enthusiast, nature is a common theme in a majority of my photographs. I am very thankful that my home is such an amazing place to photograph.

DONAHOO, BRIAN
Yosemite National Park is a cold, deserted place in the winter. The sun passes over the valley wall early in the day, casting long, icy shadows. Mixed with the roar of the falls, I could hear the ice after it broke from the top of the falls, crashing on the rocks below. The air was cold, allowing the falls to create its own snow, widening the veil. The oak, sleeping through winter, gains life-sustaining water from the mist of Bridal Veil Falls.

DONZE, CARL STEVEN
Amanda is a quirky, fun-loving seven-year-old. She has already learned to live life to the fullest. She always brings joy to the day-to-day routine of our lives.

DOWDY, KELLY M.
This is a photo of my granddaughter at the wedding of her mother and wonderful stepfather. She is two years old and made a beautiful flower girl, as you can see. I would like to dedicate the publication of this photo to my brother-in-law, Hubert L. Posey, a very talented artist and poet. We will miss you terribly.

DOWN, ANDY
This photo was one of many shot at the Air and Sea Show, held in Ft. Lauderdale, Florida, in honor of those serving in the United States Armed Forces.

DUNN, JOHN E.
John Dunn was born and raised in California. He has been an art director for over twenty-five years. His photo specialty is to find the extraordinary in the ordinary. Here in "Curious Christmas," he found his grandson, Zack, exploring Christmas decorations on a huge tree. The photo was taken in an outdoor mall in beautiful Santa Barbara, California. The picture reflects Dunn's specialty; an ordinary, curious child in an ordinary mall, caught in an extraordinary position, exploring what we all may take for granted.

DUPREE, WILLIAM L.
I am an avid nature photographer specializing in insects. There were hundreds of these dragonflies flying over the Suwannee River in southern Georgia. I had to get a couple of shots of them. I found a spot where they were perching and returned later to photograph them. It was about a two-mile hike to the spot. I spotted several perched along the bank and was able to capture their delicate beauty.

EDMUND, ALLY C.
I was in Seattle, Washington, for just one day when I decided to take some pictures with my new camera. My grandmother, Mildred Edmund, purchased it for me. I love driving dump trucks for a living and in my spare time, I take pictures and play with my pit bull named Chopper. The buildings in Seattle are amazing; the architects that are responsible must have been very artistic, not to mention incredibly intelligent.

ELLSWORTH, JEAN

This is our beautiful great-granddaughter, Yvonne (Von-Von for short). She spent a lot of time with our bird, Chatter Box, and they became good friends. When Chatter Box landed on her shoulder it made for a beautiful picture. Von-Von and her brothers, Robert and Richard, all love animals.

EMRICH, STEVE

My son, Jacob, was born on January 1, 2006. This picture was taken at our home two weeks later. He was sitting on my lap, ready for his dinner, while Mom was making up his bottle. He just couldn't wait and grabbed the closest thing to his mouth, my nose. Our friend, Karen, just happened to be there with her camera ready and snapped the shot.

ESACOVE, ADAM SETH

This is a photo of my daughter, Isabella. It was taken at our friend's family picnic. Isabella is our only child and was four months old at the time. She brings joy to our family every day. My wife, Renee, has a framed copy of this picture on her desk at work. It is a constant reminder of what is truly important in life.

ESPARZA, RONNIE L.

This is our dog, Lola; she's an ornery little dog. When it rains, or when she feels like it, she'll kick Bonita, a golden lab, out of her doghouse and take over. On this particular day, it stormed all night! Well, Bonita didn't give up her doghouse this time and Lola wouldn't stay in hers, so here is the result of consequence. For this, we got the "mad dog" look from her next morning. So, I couldn't help it and had to catch her look on camera.

ESPINOSA, TRACY

This picture was taken outside Antigo, Wisconsin, one day after the first snowfall of the season.

FELIX, CRISTY MARIE

"White Serenity" was taken near my home in Hereford, Arizona. It is a sight that we don't see very often. The chapel, Our Lady of the Sierras, is located on top of a mountain in beautiful southern Arizona. I was standing outside my home right after it snowed, I looked up and there it was. To me, this photo lets us all know that we will be all right and that there is always peace after the storm.

FINN, SUSAN M.

This picture was taken in Campus Martius Park, Detroit. This was the first Super Bowl in about twenty years or more that Detroit hosted. It was a spectacular evening with friends who are also photo enthusiasts. What a great night it was!

FLATTER, YVONE

I look for the beauty in nature to share with people and that is why I enjoy taking pictures. I have experienced both highs and lows in my life. There is a lot of ugly in the world today, but I wanted to let people know and see that beauty still exists. I thank God for giving me the talent to be able to see the beauty, and show it to you.

FONTAINE CASEY, DORIS J.

My husband, Tom, and I went house hunting in the mountains of Colorado. As we were driving on a dirt road, an animal crossed in front of us. Our realtor stopped the car and, to our amazement, there was a bobcat! He stopped and turned around to look at us. I reached for my camera and with no time to waste, I clicked three times. The bobcat ran away. We were ecstatic to see him on the third picture! This is the best picture I have ever taken, and under pressure at that!

FONTENOT, MADELINE

A couple of hours can seem like an eternity to a two-year-old while waiting for his mommy to return. I took this picture of my grandson, Blaise, while he was walking around the yard. He stopped next to the fence and was just starring down the road. It captures the innocence of a child waiting and hoping that the next car will be his mom's.

FOSHEE, ANNETTE

I took this picture in Key West, Florida, while on vacation. When we visited the outside area of the aquarium, I saw this bird overlooking one of the ponds that housed large fish. I thought it was funny how the bird was watching them so intensely and I just had to capture it. Taking pictures is one of the most relaxing things I like to do. My favorite types of pictures are landscapes and animals.

FRASER, HARRY M.

This is a picture of my granddaughter at Daytona Beach, Florida. A low camera position made it possible to capture the reflection off the sand.

FRENCH, CONSTANCE PATRICIA

This is a photo of my dog, Badger. I had some beautiful mums and a pumpkin on my front porch, and I thought it would make such a great photo. I love to take pictures of Badger and all of the people that I love. It allows me to be surrounded by them every day.

FUERSICH, AIDA

One morning I awoke and stepped out onto my deck, overlooking the Catskill Mountains. My breath was taken away by the beauty and cotton-like softness of the clouds. They seemed to whisper, "They sky is the limit."

FURMANSKAYA, ALEKSANDRA

This is a photo of my son, Victor. I also have a daughter, Anna. They are our inspiration for everything we do and, of course, for photography. My husband and I take pictures very often. Family photos are the way to illustrate family history, events, major milestones, and moments of happiness. We like to capture moments that make the pictures alive and this photo is one of them. Victor just got the new activity center. He was turning and spinning, playing with toys, and smiling for me, and the moment was captured forever!

GARDZINA, BARBARA

I am from Cracow, Poland, a very famous and historical place and the site of many kings. Cracow became a meeting place of many cultures and nations, and has successfully claimed its position as a city of culture, art, and science. I've studied at the Agricultural University of Cracow. I took part in a student exchange program with Purdue University in Indiana. My big love is to travel. Over the past years, I have traveled through Europe, western Asia, and northern Africa. Photography gives me an opportunity to catch some of those magic moments.

GARFIELD, KELLY

This picture was a spur of the moment idea. My friend, Hannah, has long hair, really long hair! So, we pulled it forward and turned her into a man. I snapped the photo and we almost died of laughter. As an aspiring filmmaker, I always have a camera handy!

GARLAND, TAMMY LYNNE

This is a photo of my then six-month-old granddaughter, Danica Shea. She is Grandma and Grandpa's pride and joy. Her mother, Jessica, and I have fun taking pictures of this precious child.

GERMAN, EMMALYN CARTER

When I noticed Fluffy under the umbrella the morning after a big rainstorm, I ran for the camera and hoped she would hold her pose until I could capture the moment. Thank you, Fluffy, for waiting for me! I would love to be an artist and oil paint, but I never seem to find the time and space for it. I have discovered I can take digital photos and fulfill some of those artistic dreams.

GIANNINI, DAWN B.

This is a picture of my daughter, Marie. She and her brother constantly bring joy into my life. I am a proud stay-at-home mother that is blessed to have a hardworking, dedicated husband, and father to my children. This picture was taken on a hike in Tahoe, California, while her father was on a two-week family leave from serving our country overseas. Marie needed to sit down and rest. She was debating if she wanted to continue or not, enjoy.

GIFT, WENDY P.

This photo was taken at a flower show I attended. I was taking a photo class at the time and trying to look at things from a new perspective. I absolutely love taking nature pictures. I also am an independent consultant for Creative Memories. I would like to thank Andy D'Angelo for teaching me how to properly get the best from my camera. My husband says I take too many photos, but you never know if you are capturing the best if you take just one.

GODSEY, MONTY A.

Being raised on the Oregon coast, I found it a little ironic taking this sunset picture while in Maui, Hawaii. I would like to thank my sister-in-law, Alice. I would also like to dedicate this photo to her, my mother-in-law, Yvonne, and of course, to my mother, Mary.

GONZALEZ, ELENA

This man's pensive and hopeful pose caught my eye while at Boca Chica Beach in the Dominican Republic. As the tropical sun slowly retreated, his mode of standing provoked in me a sense of admiration, determination, and inquiry into the purpose of life. I admired his sense of determination as he strolled up and down the beach hoping to sell his coconuts. I always remind my children that intelligence without discipline is nothing. I advise them that they must work hard for the things they want in life. Even the less fortunate can teach us that determination and hope go hand in hand.

GOODRICH, RACHEL
This is Santa's Christmas present to Brandon and me! My daughter, Tara, was sitting in her swing looking at herself in the toy mirror. She was going crazy laughing at herself for about ten minutes. I love taking pictures and I am so happy I captured this wonderful memory. I look at this picture and find myself laughing. This is one little girl that is full of laughs and smiles. This is the best Christmas present Santa could have given us!

GRABER, JOSEPH DANIEL
I took this picture of my niece holding one of our Shih Tzu puppies. She looked so sweet holding it that I couldn't resist taking this photo. My niece is five years old and the puppy was eight days old. I don't know if there's anything more precious than a child and their pet.

GRAHAM, TERESA
This is my husband's favorite picture of our daughter, Kiera, at ten months old. I captured this moment during one of her ordinary days, playing with her toys. What makes it even more special is that Kiera is wearing the same sweater I wore at her age. This is one of our favorite photos and Kiera is absolutely Daddy's girl.

GRAVES, RAFEAL DERMUNDO
I love God's gift of beauty in nature, animals, and people. It shows how creative the great Creator has been over the ages. When I look through a camera lens, I try to capture in nature what He has created. This photo is of a gorilla laid back with a smile, watching me as I "monkey around" with the camera.

GRIFFIN, CANDISE STEVEN
"Beyond Beauty" reminds me of the trials of reaching your goals. The barbed wire represents the outside influences that hinder you from reaching your goals. The sunset is the pinnacle of your goal.

GRISCHKAT, JASON
While on vacation visiting my father in Missouri, my brother and I went hiking through the many cliffs and steeps of the rolling terrain. That is where I snapped this picture "Mossy Creek." I've always felt that nature is artistry at its best. There is so much beauty in our national parks and forests across the United States. I highly recommend that everyone get out there and see our great land.

GUENTHER, TIA
My camera is always in my purse! I am always taking pictures of everything. "Maui Harbor Sunrise" was taken while I was on patrol for my security job. The colors of this sunrise were so illuminating; I had to capture it for the world to see!

GUERRERO, YOSETH
I took this picture on the way back to Los Angeles, coming from Santa Maria. I, along with my friends Terri, Melanie, Ali, Sean, and Ryan, decided to stop by the beach. We got out of the car to stretch and I became overwhelmed by the most relaxing sunset I've ever seen. As I looked out into the ocean, I couldn't help but think how beau-

tiful the horizon was. I wanted to remember that feeling forever.

GUTIERREZ, ANDRES M.
Photography is new to me. I recently discovered how much I enjoy taking pictures while on a business trip to Asia. I took this picture in the early evening as I was walking out to my office. It had just rained and there was so much rich wet color, I couldn't help myself. Living in San Francisco has inspired me to develop photography into a hobby, and maybe one day, a career. There is so much life in this city; it is difficult not to be overcome by it.

GUYNUP, ELISSA
While visiting an indigenous community in Nayarit, Mexico, we visited an elementary school. Always eager to smile for the camera, the children were adorable. This was taken because it was such a contrast to what I usually see. But, smiling is the one universal language found among these children.

HALE, AMBER
This is my beautiful baby girl, Adrianna Starr, posing for her first Valentine's Day (2006) at one month old. She is such an adorable and sweet little baby doll. I love her with all my heart and soul; she is my world. Everyone thinks she is a baby doll because of her beauty and personality.

HALLIDAY, SHANE DEAN
I recently retired after thirty-four years with the Halifar Regional Police in Novia Scotia, Canada. I have always enjoyed photography and now I have the time. Ted, "the poster cat," is my kitty that lives with his mom in Ottawa, Canada. He is an indoor cat that is very patient when there is a camera around. In this photo Ted is saying, "Here I am, how do you like me?"

HARBLIN, CONNI ANN
This is a photo of my husband, Gary, with our then two-year-old granddaughter, Mya. Mya wanted to hold the little tree frog, but was very hesitant to do so. I took this photo knowing it was a one-in-a-million shot. This photo has already gotten an honorable mention and was placed on display with the winners of an art show in the State College Art Gallery.

HARRINGTON, ROBERT DEAN
This is a photo of Newport Beach, California. A spring storm rolling in from the Pacific added to the drama and color of the sky. It was a beautiful day I will always remember.

HARRISON, CRYSTAL
This is a photo of my son, Leroy. He loves French fries, but was so tired that he fell asleep with one in his mouth. When he woke up, he still ate the fry. I took this picture to capture a moment I wanted to remember, and to share with family and friends. I love to take pictures of my children, my family, and my friends. I almost always have my camera with me for those moments in life that should be captured and forever remembered.

HARTLEY, JANA LAVONNE
Holly Hartley was born August 17, 2000. Holly

was just eight months old in this portrait. Whimsy and delight are accurate words to portray my reaction to having a baby daughter. This portrait depicts those feelings perfectly. The title, "I Do Believe I Can Fly," is a direct reference to her personality!

HEFLIN, JANE MARIE
Behind me is the busy noise and meaningless issues of the corporate milieu. Behold a different world at the monastery in Ireland. There is a wonder about this place and the glory of God's creation. The soothing silence and peace is reflective of my soul, yet caught in an eternal glimpse!

HENSON, TRACEY JEAN
My ambition is to succeed in the vast world of professional photographers. I believe this image of Tom is a breakthrough. People from foreign countries can be quite challenging. When I captured Tom in this image, I was delighted. We were chatting (the best we could due to the language barrier) and drinking kava in a small village near Nadi, Fiji. The atmosphere was relaxed and comfortable, which enable me to capture a natural, almost candid moment in time. I am very proud of this photograph.

HERR, JENNY LYNN
This photo was taken along the highway in Irish Beach, California. I love the way the water swirls around the rocks and how green the water is. The water was that color of green and blue all along the highway.

HERRERA, JACK
The photo we submitted is of just one of our many pets, his name is Jack. My wife and I were celebrating our Spurs spirit here in San Antonio, Texas. Jack has been a part of our lives for the last three years. My wife found him on her way home for lunch. We searched for his owners, but nobody claimed him. We feel so lucky nobody came forward to claim him, because he is such a big part of our lives. We can't imagine life without Jack.

HILL, HELEN MARIE
My family loves taking pictures; we all enjoy taking photos of family and friends. I especially enjoy outdoor images: beautiful sunsets, a tree's reflection on water, and weathered barns. This rose was taken while on an outing with a friend and fellow shutterbug.

HOBDY, CANDICE
I am starting to take photography serious, so I am very pleased and honored to be published in this elegant book. I have always loved to take photos. I see photos as a way of capturing history. You always remember something about the day a photo was taken that makes you smile, laugh, cry, or even upset. You remember the lesson you may have learned that day as well. This photo was taken on a mini road trip to San Francisco. It was two days before the New Year (2006) and it was beautiful. It was a day I will never forget.

HOFACKER, SARAH LOUISE
This is a photo of my granddaughter, Takylah. This is the second spring I have taken her picture in the same flowerbed; I think it will become an

annual event. I noticed this year how difficult it was to keep her interested in the flowers. I am a true amateur photographer; "Spring In Bloom" was pure luck. I will surely cherish it forever.

HOLLIDAY, KENNETH
This photo was taken on the southern rim of the Grand Canyon in early July.

HOOVER, JANETTE ANN
I'm always looking for the opportunity to capture a unique picture. This sunflower seeded itself in my flowerbed. Although it began to tower above my other flowers, I didn't have the heart to pull it out. It became so full of seeds its head bent forward and faced the other flowers below. It was late in the afternoon last fall when I took the picture. I sat on the ground and pointed my camera upward. The sun began to set, creating a beautiful pink-blue background and thus, "Sunflower Sky" was born.

HOUGHTON, ELKE
This photograph was taken along the coast of California. My daughter served as my model. I have been hooked on photography ever since I got my very own camera at the age of seven. To me, photography is a wonderful way to express my feelings about what I see and experience. Photography has changed the way I sense the world around me. It has taught me to draw in every moment by learning to see, feel, and discover life itself, and the beauty it has to offer. By looking through the camera's eye, each moment touches my soul.

HOUSTON-MCMILLAN, ANDREW
One often hears of nature's beauty; this photo is a confirmation of God's creation. Sometimes one is at the right place at the right time. This was one of those moments in scenic Elora, Ontario, Canada. I captured the picture while taking a stroll on a fresh winter's day in the gorge. This picture is proof that unspoiled nature still exists.

HOWARD, KAY
Fraulein, my 137-pound Doberman pinscher, is an eating machine. It is not uncommon for her to wake up crunching the cookie left dangling from her lips as she fell asleep the night before. She loves chicken and rice, and her daily "fix" consists of a pound of assorted treats. She can hold an ear of corn between her paws and strip off every kernel. Fraulein's favorite lunch is potted meat, spread between two slices of bread, with a large bowl of ice cream for dessert.

HOWELLS, KRISTINA JEAN
Looking out of the window on a cold winter's day, snow lying all around, I snuggle up to a hot chocolate. The photo is about purity. The snow on the ground represents this. The photograph was taken from the apartment that I share with my fiancé, Frank. It is an image of winter that I will remember. I am a teacher and I love sharing ideas with my students. Frank is a keen photographer like me and we enjoy going out together and taking photographs.

HUDSON, GLEN F.
As an amateur photographer I have always seen life through the lens of a camera, whether it be nature, people, events, or occurrences. I like to look beyond, see what is really there, and bring it to life with my camera. This photo is of cherry blossoms in full bloom in my backyard at the end of April this year.

HUNT, SHANNON DELLA
I live in the county with this fantastic view. I took this photo from our back deck. I like how the sun is shining in the middle of the field, with all the different shades of green. The object that looks like a ladder in the bottom left corner is actually a hag wagon. I just started taking an interest in photography this past year. I am enjoying taking pictures of the scenery, and I also take a lot of pictures of my family and pets.

INKOL, DOUGLAS J.
My wife, Nancy, and I lived and worked in Malta, a small country in the Mediterranean Sea, for several years where we pioneered a successful chiropractic practice. During that time, we had the opportunity to visit and explore several European countries. This photo inspired me while visiting the south of France. It was a gorgeous, warm, and sunny day. We were enjoying the scenery when I captured Nancy eating the best part of her ice cream cone with the historical scenery of Saint Tropez in the background. It was a most memorable moment and a beautiful day in Saint Tropez!

ISABEL, TREVOR
This was my first nighttime photograph. It was so rewarding to me in print. Nighttime photography has become a fun, creative expression for me.

ISHMAEL, DON R.
I am interested in how science and art interplay. Science studies and attempts to explain nature, meanwhile art represents and reproduces nature. I like the exact representation of nature as photography. I like to use old techniques and explore prints, but I also like to use oils to paint, as well as computer-generated manipulations. Sometimes I like to put together montages of all the techniques. I like to explore nature and the natural phenomenon around me. I also like to explore people.

JACKSON, KIMBERLY ANN
I chose this photo because my son loves bubbles. We play with bubbles just about every day. His nice smile and the clear shot of the bubbles just made a peaceful picture. He's a miracle child and I love sharing his smile with everyone.

JAUCH, KIMBERLY RENEE'
Inspiration can hit anyone at any moment. When you are able to catch it, it becomes priceless. This inspiration hit me as the mountains became covered in a beautiful white snow. Jazy's nose turned white after her journey to find her beloved treasure, her tennis ball. This simple task led to my capturing this perfect journey. Now, it is forever captured on film, along with our hearts.

JENNINGS, STEPHEN PAUL
This is a rare sight of an octopus outside of its hole. Even more rare is that this particular octopus, all six feet of it, just sat there, seemingly carefree of my presence. Even when I was within three feet, he would not move from the coral. I take hundreds of photos of many different sea creatures all around the world, especially here in Hawaii.

JOHNSON, KRISTINA
"To the world you are a soldier, to me you are my world." This picture was taken minutes before he left for Afghanistan. My husband is a great soldier and a wonderful father. I am very proud of him and what he is doing for our country. I love you, Sgt. Johnson.

JOHNSON, WALLY
I am humbled and appreciative to have been selected for this honor. Having bought the camera to be able to take and send images of antiques to dealers and collectors, I never envisioned using it for this purpose. I feel very fortunate to have come upon this one moment in time, a moment when all the ingredients of color and contrast produced such a delightful result. It has become my desire to capture many more of these precious moments.

JORDAN, JESSICA
I am a student at Hillsborough Community College. In high school I studied film, and also was a part of the closed circuit television programming for our school. Last year, I got an opportunity to go into the photography field and work for a studio. I am enjoying it and learning a great deal in the process. The title of my self-portrait is "Mirror." This shows the very soul of who I am, nothing to hide as an artist, vulnerability.

JURESH, TARA L.
I took this picture of my daughter while she was in her wrestling singlet. She has a couple of her first place medals on. This was her first year wrestling and she ended the season with twelve wins and three losses. She was never pinned. There are people out there who believe a girl can't and shouldn't wrestle. To all of them, I'd like to say, "I beg to differ."

KAVANAUGH, PEACHES
I took this photo on a "beautiful fall day in Ohio" last year, while a friend and I were hiking in a park, enjoying the crisp, cool air. We came upon this scene by a gurgling river, and the sight took our breath away. I fumbled quickly for my camera, hoping to record the beauty of the occasion. As luck would have it, the camera seemed to capture the essence of that wonderful moment in Mother Nature's awesome portfolio. I'm pleased that this nature scene was considered worthy enough to share with a larger audience.

KELLEY, CANTRIECE SHAVELLE
This photo of my cousin, Christina, and me was taken at a playground. Christina and I have always been best cousins, we have so much love for each other. I feel as though she's my "lucky star." Due to school, we see each other less. We decided to take a picture, just in case one misses the other. That way, we can daydream about all the fun we have had together.

KELLY, KRYSTAL ROSE
Being the horse-enthusiast that I am, I couldn't stop myself from capturing this horse on film. This little pony was kept in a disgusting-looking

paddock, up to his fetlocks in mud. It was the eyes that caught my attention the most. Of all the horses located on this property in California, this pony had the most expressive eyes. I have my own thoroughbred horse named Thunder. I have been training Thunder for almost two years now. I am a student and I ride in my spare time.

KENDLE, RICK LEE
Thank you for this opportunity; it has enabled me to share my love for life. I am in charge of an out-reach ministry in Springfield, Virginia. My prayer is to be able to share the beauty that God has given to us. Someone had just eaten a banana on the beach and discarded the empty peel. A white-faced monkey saw the peel lying on the beach and jumped down to grab it. Unfortunately, the banana was gone!

KETCHUM, JUDY ANN
This has been a fun experience. I'm grateful to have the opportunity to share a favorite photo with others. Most of my photography is of macro flow-ers that can be seen on my web site at www.judyannschaller.com. Later this year, I will have a coffee table book available.

KIFER, BRENDA ARLENE
Living life in the critical care setting as a nursing assistant, vacation is always welcomed. Recently, we visited Las Vegas, Nevada, and were fortunate enough to be able to take a ride through the Valley of Fire! While there, I shot this tranquil photo of the various scenes of beau-ty. The red rocks, plus the mountains and clouds, framed a lasting picture in my mind, and I'm so glad I captured its beauty on camera.

KING, VICKIE
As a handler with American Search Dogs, I get to spend a lot of time in my beloved mountains. Never going anywhere without my camera, I have had countless opportunities to catch nature at its best. I have developed a great love and respect for the moose, the gentle giant of the forest. I have learned the habitat of many, and watched them grow while living in peace all around them. This young bull cautiously watched my dog while I took several photos. Then we each went our way, glad to have crossed paths.

KINSAUL, RAYMOND EDWARD
This is a helicopter as it breaks ground, heading back to its home base. It is not a good idea to use a flash while photographing an aircraft at night because it interferes with the pilot's night vision. I got permission to use the flash for this picture while they were taking off. The pilot, Tom Zuber, and I have been longtime friends; we lived across the street from each other as teenagers. The result is this beautiful mixture of colors, glowing in the night, as the helicopter leaps up into the air.

KIRKENDALL, DANIEL T.
"Goldilocks And The Polar Bear" is a picture of my daughter, Kami, and the polar bear, her friend at Sea World in San Diego, California. Although others observed the polar bear, he would rarely come to the glass until Kami appeared. They seem to have an affinity. My dad and I have always loved the water, fishing, and all things

ocean. Kami seems to have inherited that gene. She caught her first fish at two years; it weighed what she weighed at birth.

KLEIN, DANIEL EDWARD
Being retired allows me the time to travel, which gives me the opportunity to photograph scenic sights. This panoramic portrait of the sunrise was taken while waiting for the ferry to go from Orient Point, New York, to New London, Connecticut. As the sun ascended from beyond the horizon, it appeared to set the ocean and sky on fire.

KOPCZEWSKI, MARK JOHN
This picture was taken while at a park. Georgia is the eldest of three grandchildren. I am forty-seven years old and have been married to my wife, Carol, for twenty-seven. We have two children: Cheryland and Marek. I am self-employed and have only recently taken up photography.

KRATZ, DEBRA EILEEN
I drove across the United States last year to take my son to college. There were so many beautiful sights, but the most breathtaking was the Grand Canyon. It was truly a beautiful sight to see. I look forward to capturing more of these natural sights this year as we take a different route to visit my son.

KRIEGER, DELIA C.
My husband and I decided to have our honey-moon at the Big Island of Hawaii. On our way to visiting one of the tropical gardens, we came across this unique image of vines coming down like strings on a harp. We had never seen anything quite like it. When traveling, we always bring our camera. It is a good way to remember special moments together.

KRONSHAGE, MATT
I find capturing nature with a camera inspiring and fulfilling; it makes me feel so free. I would like to become a professional photographer some-day. This photo was taken at Camp Pendleton in Escondido, California. I love sunsets, especially on the ocean. They make me feel relaxed, like the world is frozen in that very moment, just waiting for me to take the picture. This photo is probably my best yet. This picture will be an inspiration to me forever.

KRUSE, DEB
This is a very special little girl named Kyra Leigh, my first granddaughter, and the pride and joy of my life. Her mommy, Amy, is a wonderful mother and very special daughter-in-law. Her daddy, Parker, is a wonderful father and the best son any mother could ask for. Parker arrived home from Afghanistan just two weeks prior to Kyra's birth in September 2005. He's been work-ing in Iraq for the past six months and I know Mommy and Kyra miss him terribly. We keep Dad informed of his daughter's progress through these wonderful photographs.

LACKIE, JAMES
This photo was taken in Arbroath, Scotland, when my wife, Helena, and I were on our retirement trip around the globe in 2005. It was a bit of a fluke as the planes only passed once at high speed and I had just recently started photography as a retirement

hobby. I was thrilled with the outcome at that time, but even more so now that somebody else thinks it is a good picture. The aircraft are part of the Royal Air Force Red Arrows display team.

LAGOMARSINO, JACK
One morning, I poured myself a glass of seltzer and dropped in two slices of lime. I then went into the television room and set the glass on the coffee table before returning to the kitchen for a snack. When I came back to the room and reached for the glass of seltzer, I noticed how the sunlight passing through the window made the seltzer bubbles and limes take on a "glow." Wanting to preserve that moment, I grabbed my camera and this photo is the result.

LAMAR, AMBER
I recently traveled with a group of students and teachers from People to People Student Ambassador Programs. We visited France, Italy, and Malta. France was such an awesome place and it was a wonderful experience. I wanted to share a piece of that with everyone else. When you take a picture it is like you capture a moment that you will never forget. Going to these differ-ent countries was a great cultural experience and I think this photograph shows just that.

LAMB, DAVID W.
Throughout my life, I have always wanted to be a photographer. I imagined taking the photos and developing my own pictures, then came digital cameras. My dear mother bought me a Sony Cybershot 2.1 MP. Since that time, I've taken over fifteen thousand photos. I have captured my life in those photos over the last few years. Timeless is the best way I could describe my love of photography. "Things Are Looking Up" is a picture of a cave, nestled in the hills of Tennessee.

LAMPARD, CLETUS LEE
This is a photo of my daughter and grandson, watching the sunset in Aruba. It was the first time I have ever been there; it was a nice relaxing time and I would love to be there again. I am seventy-six years old, but I work all winter at the local ice rink. I do a lot of repairs and sometimes drive the Zamboni. I also paint, draw, and take photographs in order to take my mind off the world's problems. Some people do not take the time to look at how very lovely the world is. So many things go unno-ticed and pictures capture those moments, so we can remember them forever.

LANDERS, SONYA
Spring is one of my favorite times of the year; it signifies new beginnings. Spring is the time of year when everything seems brighter and more colorful. In my picture, I tried to capture the essence of spring. I am a mother of four, plus a nephew. And just like all others, I ride the roller coaster of life at full speed. I think we sometimes forget to take the time to enjoy and admire the simplistic beauty that surrounds us.

LAW, KERRI L.
Madeline has always been a fan of an American icon, the teddy bear. As a kitten she would carry around a teddy, given to my husband, Steve, by his daughter. We soon learned this little bear no

longer belonged to him. At night, Madeline would bring the bear to bed, and during the day she would carry it back down the stairs to the living room. It was almost as if it, too, was a part of our family. Madeline will always love bears, and this snapshot of her hanging out with her "friends" makes me wonder if the bears are thinking about what they would do without a friend like her.

LAWRENCE, TIMOTHY JAMES
This photo was taken on my trip to France. Our tour coach stopped at this spot for a great photo opportunity. This is my favorite picture from the trip, by far. It provides a spectacular view of the crystal-clear Mediterranean, the dramatic landscape, and celebrity estates on the hillside. When submitting my photo for this contest, I had two choices: this one and a picture overlooking Sydney Harbor. Although spectacular, the other photo lacks clarity and has been seen too often. I'm working on getting this picture enlarged, so I can frame it and cherish it forever.

LAYMAN, TERI LYNNE
I took this picture while I was on a dental mission trip in Guyana, South America. We got to fly into the rainforest and hiked to see this amazing waterfall. It is Kaieteur Falls, one of the longest waterfalls in the world, dropping over seven hundred feet. It was absolutely breathtaking and an experience I will never forget!

LEEUW, CAROLYNN M.
A unique moment occurred when this butterfly fluttered from the October sky, regally settling on a clump of pansies. I am not a great nature photographer — my first preference is taking photos of individuals. I'm a parenting trainer who works with families experiencing many difficulties. My camera is the best work tool I have. I take pictures of the families and give them copies. The photos do wonders for self-esteem building and become unique moments in the lives of these families. So, the click of my camera does more than preserve memories, it also brings enjoyment and hope.

LEINGANG, CHANTRY I.
This is a picture of my daughter, Marissa M. Leingang. This is her first time ever seeing a duck; she laughed so hard I had to take the picture. Thank you for choosing my picture for this book.

LESKY, CINDY L.
My grandfather, Elroy Nelson, loved to take pictures. He had a real knack for it and I guess he passed it on. My daughter, Ashley, and I were renting a cottage on Waubeesee Lake in Wisconsin. The cottage wasn't the greatest, but the view was everything. "Family Time" was taken at sunrise. It represented the sign I was looking for, a new day and a new start. I loved the view from that cottage.

LEWIS, DAVID EUGENE
This photo was taken during a business trip to Pittsburgh, Pennsylvania. It was taken from Mount Washington, prior to Three Rivers Stadium being torn down. The Pirates had just beat the Phillies on a Saturday night. I have worked with several people from the Pittsburgh area, and heard of some of the outstanding views in the area. I

never imagined I would be fortunate enough to have gotten this opportunity.

LEWIS, DUSTIN
I took this photo from the hanger bay on the USS Kitty Hawk (CV-63) in the spring of 2003. Our mission consisted of over one hundred days in the Persian Gulf, with no liberty ports. After working between sixteen and twenty hours a day, seven days a week, for that long, depression eventually sets in. I woke up one morning around five, after only a couple of hours of sleep, to work and I found this sunrise. Stunned, I ran back to get my camera, knowing the amazing scene would only last for moments. This picture lifted my spirits when I needed it most. My father, Orville William Lewis III, is an amazing photographer, and has inspired me to keep my eye out for that picture-perfect moment. So, Dad, I dedicate this photo to you.

LINDNER, SARAH ELIZABETH
This is a photo of the Drum Corps International World Championship Finals 2005, held in Gillette Stadium. I am a member of the front ensemble of the Boston Crusaders Drum and Bugle Corps, shown here preparing for our last show of the summer. The 135-member corps spends three months together over the summer, playing music, competing, and touring the United States. I made so many friends and gained so many great memories over the summer. It has been the most meaningful experience of my life, so far.

LIPIRO, BOB
After a hurricane passed Sanibel Island, Florida, in July 2005 the Gulf calmed down and the sky lit up with this setting sun.

LITTERAL, JUSTINA
I received a new digital camera and was bored while coming back from a school meeting. I started taking pictures of my cousin and myself in our car. From the pictures I had taken, my family and friends told me that this picture caught the beauty of my eyes.

LOCKHART, PATSY ANN
This is a photo of my daughter, Emily Ann. When I tried this outfit on her, she looked like a little lady. Her eyes and face show the innocence of a child, and how children really do depend on us as parents. This child is truly a gift from God. Her daddy calls her "Princess." I call her "Miss Emily," sometimes because there is no doubt in my mind, she will be the boss, or at least think so.

LOOKER, GARY EDWARD
I have always loved photography. I tend to take my camera everywhere because you never know when inspiration will hit. This photo was taken on a vacation with my wife. The picture inspires feelings of a different era, when life was much simpler. This picture reminds us to slow down and enjoy life.

LOVING, RON
I've had a love for photography ever since my father gave me a Brownie camera when I was eight years old. Over the years, my love and passion for photography has grown. I love the outdoors and love to photograph what Mother Nature

has given us. I wish I could capture all the beauty this world has to offer. There are beautiful, interesting images everywhere!

LUDAS, GERALDINE
I took this picture while watching this squirrel lick our birdbath as if she had an itch on her tongue. I feel I was born with a camera in my hand. I take family and nature pictures constantly, especially when my husband, Michael, and I are visited by our wonderful, loving family members.

LUKENS REED, DAPHNE
This photo of my daughter and her friend was taken while en route to Dallas, Texas. I looked at them in the back of the car and could not resist capturing the moment. I will always cherish it, I hope others enjoy the picture as well.

LUNDBERG, ANNE MARIE
This photo was taken in early March. My sister, brother-in-law, and I decided to avoid the winter rains and soak up the Arizona sun. Midway through our journey, we headed to Canyon de Chelly National Monument on the Navajo Indian Reservation. We arrived late in the afternoon and decided to visit the canyon the following morning. Imagine our surprise when we awoke and discovered our car covered with snow. Undaunted by the snow or wind, we trooped on and were well rewarded. The snow contrasted magnificently with the red sandstone canyon walls, creating a photographer's delight and a memorable journey indeed.

LUNDEEN, KAYLA
This picture is of Lucy. She is a West Highland terrier. Lucy loves to sleep on the end table. My brother, Alex, my sisters, Teyana and Nikaya, my mom, Shannon, and my stepfather, Doug, love to visit her. We get to see her almost every day. I love watching Lucy grow. I'm lucky to live ten minutes from them. My favorite things are animals and my favorite animals are dogs. I'd like to become a vet, so I can help animals of all kinds.

LUPOLI, PATRICIA
This was taken one very cold, snowy day in Jackson Hole, Wyoming. These trumpeted swans have found a home at the National Elk Refuge there. I spent an hour in the wet snow to shoot this beautiful bird. I have spent the last five years shooting the wonders of nature that surround us. Photography is my passion. Nothing pleases me more than to look through my viewfinder and see a natural work of art, right before my eyes.

LYLE, SHARON ANN
This photo was taken at Hill House Farms in Millstone, New Jersey. On a crisp autumn Sunday, I walked about this lovingly-restored farm, camera in hand. I took several pictures at this beautiful place, but this was my favorite. I mostly take pictures for enjoyment and to capture nature. I have never entered a photo contest before. Most of my photos go to friends and family, or hang in my house. I am truly honored to have my photograph selected for publication.

MADDEN, AMANDA
This priceless photograph is from the day my little brother, Thomas, returned from the war in Iraq.

The fear and sadness his sacrifices induced in our family were indescribable, but nothing compares to the overwhelming pride and joy we experienced upon his safe return home. Here, our niece, Alexandra, age six, accurately portrays these emotions during their first embrace after seven frightening months apart. I was ecstatic to capture this cherished moment on film and I am happy to share my cherished photo, especially with other proud American families.

MALIK, HINA

Whenever we travel by road in Canada, we always encounter rain and sunshine together. These two ingredients make up rainbows. More often than not, we are without a camera, but this time on our way to Niagara Falls, I had mine. I have never seen such a perfect rainbow and combined with the falls in the background, the view was spectacular!

MARIS, ASHLEY MARIE

Already in awe of standing near the Washington Monument, I looked to the sky on a cool, brisk evening. In the middle of the darkening sky, a plane flew into view. With my camera ready, I looked once more to the escaping sun and the moving plane, and captured the picture in memory and on film.

MARKOWSKI, BRENT ALLEN

This photo was taken during the late summer as I was walking down the Grand Haven Pier in Grand Haven, Michigan. The sun was setting and I noticed how it illuminated the rose stuck in the metal frame. I immediately took several pictures in the hopes that one would turn out decent. I've been doing photography for close to a year now, although at the moment, my career lies in the construction field. I hope that this opportunity gives me the foothold I need to further myself as a photographer.

MARTIN, JANET LEE

I captured this photograph while on a trip to the Riverbanks Zoo and Garden in Columbia, South Carolina, with my spouse, Marie, and our daughter, Erika. I enjoy taking pictures of our adventures and everyday life together. Marie enjoys putting them in scrapbooks and then the memories are saved for a lifetime.

MARTYN, NEAL S.C.

Our dog, Star, is a purebred Pekingese. We bought him at a pet store. He has beautiful color tones. This picture was taken when he was only six months old, playing at the beach. We caught his attention very well in this photo. The timing of this picture was perfect. You can also see that he was eating sand. See the star on his forehead?

MASON, EILEEN R.

This photo was taken at the Nixon Farm (no relation) in Friendship, Maryland, in August 2001. I was there with my parents for a picnic and I got bored, so I went for a walk with my camera. My friends and family always tell me I'm in the wrong profession of work! I love taking pictures of animals and nature.

MASONWELLS, DENISE LORRAINE

This photograph was taken during holidays at the Gold Coast while in Queensland, Australia. The baby polar bear had just arrived at Sea World and was obviously enjoying her new environment. I have had a keen interest in photography for many years and love animal photography. I have managed to capture many extraordinary photographs over the years.

MASSIE, HOLLY C.

This is a picture of my two-and-a-half-year-old son, Eli Dale, holding his funny, older cousin, Sichey Lee. She really brings out a soft, gentle side to his all-boy personality. I love taking pictures of Eli. I am always trying to capture all of his expressions; it is fun! Plus, as he gets older, I can look back and see his years of changes and memories. I live on a ranch in Illinois, with my husband, Craig, and son, Eli. We have cattle and horses.

MAXON, KAREN K.

This is a photo of my grandson, Carter, on a nice summer day. You can see the joy on his face as he drives his tractor.

MAY, JILL M.

I've always enjoyed photography and the beauty of nature. My pets are treasures to me, giving me endless moments of joy. The purity and innocence they portray is exciting when I can capture it. If I run to get my camera, it seems that they know to sit and stay. Photography is a very relaxing and rewarding hobby, especially when you know these moments will last forever for future smiles.

MCADAMS, MEGAN

This is a photo of my nephew, Haden Connor Young, taken on a beautiful summer day at our barn. He has the sweetest smile, nature, and loving ways; he is just too sweet for words. He is holding a new baby chick and giving it sugars.

MCARTHUR, ROBERT

When I was about ten years old, my father and older brother were into photography. After observing them take pictures, develop, and print the black and whites, I became very interested. About twenty-five years ago I started photography, and now I have my own dark room. I take photos of portraits, landscapes, and flowers.

MCLAUGHLIN, JEFFREY

As a member of the United States Air Force, I have seen many beautiful sites and scenes. While walking out on the flight line one evening, I looked to the sky above and saw the most incredible sunset ever, one people would need to see to believe. This was truly the greatest scene I have ever witnessed in any of the countries I have been to. I have traveled to several while serving in the Air Force the last four-and-a-half years: England, France, Germany, Italy, Turkey, and Canada. Of all the amazing places I have seen, nothing beats what Kyrgyzstan had to offer.

MCNEILL, DANIEL B.

"The Pastel Colors Of St. Martin" was taken in October 2005. I was on my first cruise and we had three destinations: San Juan, Puerto Rico; St. Martin; and St. Thomas. I had a great time and took plenty of outstanding photographs while on this trip.

MCSHERRY, CAROL J.

My husband, Tom, and I were camping down by Lake George, Colorado. We were just getting ready to go rock hunting when I looked over at the car and noticed this butterfly. I couldn't stay away from it, so I grabbed the camera and took its picture.

MELROY, CHRISTIANE NICOLE

When I saw this flower, it just jumped out at me and I had to take a picture of it! The picture was taken in my backyard while living in Kenya; I was a missionary there in 2005. I saw the praying mantis on the back of the flower, just faintly. It took me by surprise! I love this photo — it contains so many memories. I feel so blessed to have captured such a beautiful moment in time that is now being shared with so many people.

MERRILL, GORDON WENDELL

I often look for special things to take a picture of, so that I may capture it on film in a most surprising way, and bring out the beauty of it. I enjoy sharing my photographs with family and friends. This one caught my eye.

MILAN, JULIE

Since high school, I have been interested in photography, which is now a hobby of mine. I'm not sure what turned me onto it, but I am particularly interested in sunsets. No matter where I am or what I'm doing, if there are colors in the sky, I'm there! This picture was taken in Kansas. As I was driving by, the reflection on the buildings caught my eye. This is my favorite sunset photo so far!

MILLER, CAROLYN J.

I am always amazed at the wonder on children's faces as they experience new moments. Grandpa loves to fish and has high hopes of fishing with "Little Missy." She loves life and you can see her enjoyment in her eyes. The little grub was her best friend for the day. My granddaughter, Jayna Jewel, is so fresh. I love to capture my grandchildren in innocent moments. I am a truly blessed grandma.

MILLER, LAVERNE H.

While mowing, I noticed the three raccoons scampering for a small tree, afraid of the noise from the lawnmower. With our house being nearby, I decided to leave the mower next to the tree and procure my camera. They were still climbing as I returned. Remembering some advice about taking more than one exposure, I took three images of them climbing while looking back to see if they were safe or not. I moved the mower as soon as I had finished taking pictures, so they could go on their way. I hope you enjoy this image as much as my family and friends have.

MILLER, ROBERT W.

I took this picture while riding around my neighborhood, taking in the beauty that fall brings. The sun was shining down on the golden leaves and it just caught my eye. I live in North Carolina, with my wife, Cheri, and daughter, Heather, where we enjoy all four seasons.

MILLS, KEVIN S.

This is a photo I took when my family and I went four-wheeling, outside of Marble, Colorado. We passed across Lizard Pond right before dusk and the pond was still. I always carry my camera with me in order to capture those "once-in-a-lifetime" memories. This moment was one that I was pleased to be able to capture.

MINNEY, DANIELLE MARIE

This is a picture of my son, Henry, on our vacation in Hawaii. I took the picture right after he finished saying, "I love you, Mama." I love the sweet look on his face.

MINTON, JIM

Photographing the cats at Thunderhawk Big Cat Rescue, Florida, has been my privilege for the past eight years. At the facility there is always something going on and lots of opportunities to take pictures. Kola, the lioness, was rescued with Sergeant, a lion from a petting zoo, and were kept together for security and comfort. Kola lost her mate due to a progressive central nervous system disease. She was extremely depressed. Waku Wa, the other cat in the photo, is a caring, nurturing tiger. She was moved in with Kola to help offset her depression. It worked.

MOGUILEVSKY, NURIT ANA

When I take a picture, I try to tell a story, creating a picture with its own life and capturing that magic moment. My goal is for the viewer to be able to imagine they are there, attempting to create their own story. This picture was taken in Buenos Aires, Argentina, and it displays a lot of Argentinean history.

MOLDENHAUER, ALANNA

Every week I drive out of my way to see this "turtle rock," and I am amazed at its character. I have no idea how long it has been there, comfortably watching the valley below. After the land was sold for housing development, I took this photo for fear that it would be moved to make way for a larger road. I am pleased to share it with everyone.

MONTE, RALPH A.

I was playing with my new camera and Mike agreed to be my model. I am always looking for a chance to practice with the camera. This was taken in Mike's backyard.

MOORE, AMANDA RAE

People often think of a happy place. Well this horse shows that happy places do exist. This horse is just relaxing on a beautiful day in Crescent City, California. I am a true cowgirl and know a happy horse when I see one. I take pictures for fun and have often been told that I am a natural. This is my first year entering my photos in a contest and I am pleased to know that I have an opportunity to share my moments with other people.

MOORE, WALLACE EDWIN

I have always loved photography, ever since I was a little boy. When I was in the Army overseas, I took hundreds of photographs of the beautiful countryside. In 2004 I had the great opportunity to go on an Alaskan cruise featuring four professional photographers. They taught classes and critiqued our photos. I learned a lot form them and this helped me switch to digital photography.

MORENO, ADAM

I've been involved in the arts my whole life. When I was younger, I loved to draw, paint, dance, and sing. When I went to college, I planned on studying graphic design. I switched my major to musical theatre and ended up graduating in theatre education. I am now a camp director at the Appel Farm Arts and Music Center. It was a snowy day when I snapped this photograph, using my new digital camera that I received for Christmas. I guess it must take a pretty good picture!

MORGAN, JAMES C.

My children are my world and they often give me lots of inspiration. My son, Bryce, loves fireworks and I tried to capture his curiosity of them. The sparklers in the picture are his favorite; he often stares at them, as well as the sparks, in amazement. Seeing this childlike wonder often helps me remember what the world looks like to children, and it helps me relive that wonder.

MORGENSTEIN, WILLIAM

This photo was taken in the kitchen of our Florida home. Our two grandsons are working diligently, putting together a complicated project.

MORRISON, CINDY JEAN

This photo was taken on our way home to Wyoming, from California. This particular shot is in Provo Canyon, Utah. We were, as my husband put it, "screaming down the highway," when I took this photo. I love taking pictures and, most of all, I enjoy sharing them with others.

MOSSBERGER, AMIE

I live in Golden, Colorado, with my family of six. I enjoy the many beautiful skies here in my home state. On the day this picture was taken, my oldest daughter yelled, "Mom, you need to come see the sky!" I grabbed my camera, went out the back door, and there was a beam shooting down from the sun. When I went to download "Twilight's Peace," I noticed the cross, not just the beam of light. When my father looked at the picture, he saw a face in the trees just under the cross. So, I'm sure this is a sign from up above.

MULLIER, JAMES ARTHUR

This photo is of our eldest daughter, Joanne. It was taken on impulse, while on holiday. Joanne's eyes seemed to reflect the thoughts of the moment. My wife's name is Kerrie and we have another daughter, Leora. We all enjoy the excitement of capturing lasting expressions of family life together.

MURPHY, BRIAN THOMAS

This picture was taken opening day of the Wichita Wranglers season. It was Mark Redmans' first outing after undergoing knee surgery. He led the Wranglers to a 4–0 lead before being removed in the fifth inning. Over five innings, he had six strikeouts, walked only one batter, and gave up two hits.

MURPHY, REBECCA

This photo is part of a series I worked on for an assignment. My subject was the train station in New Brunswick, New Jersey, near where I went to art school. This photo looks down from the plat-

form onto the intersection of Easton Avenue and Albany Street. Most of my photographs incorporate shadows, but very rarely people. What's most interesting to me about this image (very seldom do people notice) is the angel in the bottom left corner. It's as if both the shadow and the angel are watching over this woman. I continue to do photography and I am very honored to be published.

MURRAY, DARREN WILLIAM

I've always been interested in wildlife photography, but never thought I'd get to take one like this. I was lucky enough to catch this moment at Taronga Zoo in Sydney, Australia. It looks almost as if it was posed. As soon as the shutter closed, she walked off. One of my ambitions in life was to travel around Australia and New Zealand. The other is to be a wildlife photographer. I've achieved one and with a lot of hard work and luck, I hope to achieve the other!

NEBOZUK, ADRIAN

I have never expected to witness anything like this in real life. This is a picture of a mullet, captured by an osprey, in the Flamingo District of Everglades National Park. I always take my camera with me when I travel. "Osprey Catch Of The Day" is my favorite photograph, compared to all the other pictures I have taken in the past. I'm very happy to share this nature shot with other viewers like you. Thank you.

NEUMANN, CAROL JEAN

This is a picture of my granddaughter, Tiffany Lynn Tessmer, and me. Her mother, Amy, was showing me her garden. I bent down to show Tiffany a flower and, at four months old, you can see she already sees the beauty of life. A child brings so much beauty into our lives after they are born. She is my world.

NEVILLE, DEENA J.

This is a photo of my nephew, Avery Wilson, and our family dog, Gracie. This is a unique photo of the two of them. I love taking candid shots of my family and different scenes. We have two children: Meghan and Calie. My husband, John, and I also have another male rottweiler, George. I plan to surprise my sister, Dottie, and her husband, Ray, on Christmas 2006 with this photo of Avery and Gracie, our gentle giant.

NEWMAN, BETTE ANN

Photography is my passion; everywhere I go, my camera goes with me. I credit my interest in photography to my father. He loved taking pictures and developing them. With just one click, you can capture a beautiful picture for life. "Old Glory In The Sunset" was taken from my deck that offers magnificent views of the sunset. What could be grander than to capture it with the American flag? Being a mother of three and grandmother of seven, photos are so valuable. I have a business that helps people preserve their photos for future generations.

NEWMAN, CATHERINE ANNE

My name is Catherine Newman. I am twenty-six years old and I live in the beautiful Green Mountains of Vermont. This picture was taken at Lefferts Pond in Chittenden, Vermont. The fall colors are wonderful here. I wanted to display them in this scene, to share my love of Vermont and nature with the world!

NEWTON, WILMARIE D.
El Morro is an amazing fort located in San Juan, Puerto Rico. I took this picture on March 26, 2005 four days after my grandmother's burial in Puerto Rico. It had been five years since I was able to go back to Puerto Rico, and, even under those sad circumstances, it was just so good to be home. To this day, I can still close my eyes and hear the waves crashing against the walls of El Morro; I can smell the salt in the air and feel the wind blowing through my hair. It is such a magnificent, breathtaking place.

NGUYEN, LE
My husband, Joe, and I took this photo of our son, Ty, and our dog, Bella. In this photo, Ty is seven months old and is celebrating his very first Easter. At the right moment, we were able to photograph them quickly while glancing at each other. Unfortunately, we weren't able to take more since there was only a small window of opportunity to have Ty dressed in an Easter outfit, due to the warm weather outside. A moment like this is priceless and is captured in mere seconds, but it will remain with us for all of our lives.

NORRIS, SIMEON SHANE
I never thought that two small people could make me feel so alive, but seeing this tender moment between sisters gives the world a second chance.

NORSWORTHY, THERESA MARIE
This is a photo of my son, Devon. It was taken just after I returned from a six-month deployment in Afghanistan. Seeing him playing in the tree triggered memories of my own childhood when we enjoyed the simple pleasure of climbing trees. But, it also highlighted the disparity between the lives of children here and of those children I saw in Kabul.

O'BRIEN, ERIN E.
My family and I are able to enjoy wonderful summers in a town called Chester, Nova Scotia, Canada. I cherish my morning walks, watching the sunrise over the harbor. The view is always breathtaking and never short on interesting shots. This gorgeous backdrop makes photography easy!

OGLES, JULIE ANN
We went outside to get some pictures of Rose for St. Patrick's Day. It was slightly overcast and there were some beautiful blue hues in the sky. Instead of smiling and laughing like usual, Rose's attention was focused on the greenery and sounds of nature. I caught this one while she was staring at her father, John, who was making silly faces. She watched him so intently it makes you wonder what she was thinking.

OH, SAE
In our fast moving world, it's not always easy to appreciate the little things that surround us. Sometimes, all you have to do is change your point of view and you'll discover the truly important things in life; it may even be hiding under your dining room table.

OLGUIN, ELIZABETH
It has been said a picture paints a thousand words. This picture does just that. It is a photograph taken in 1960 of two of my nine sons: Daryl and Gregory. I am very grateful for this picture because my beloved child, Gregory, died on Christmas Eve in 1998. He was riding his bike when a car hit him. In a small way, I am honoring Gregory by sending you this meaningful picture of his endless journey.

PALLOT, LAURIE A.
I photographed this primitive tribe in their ancestral habitat, the remote and sparsely populated western Indonesia province Irian Jaya (West Papua). Lacking modern transportation and communication infrastructures fosters isolation and the existence of pre-historic societies, even in the twenty-first century. The children pictured stand in front of their family's thatched roof, earthen floored, wooden hut. The lives they lead and rituals they practice are those of their Stone Age ancestors. As civilization expands into Earth's diminishing wilderness areas, the end of such societies is foretold. I hope my photos will bear witness to future generations the existence of such societies.

PALMER, DEBORAH
This photo was taken at a miniature horse show. Ally and her horse were waiting to go in the ring and I could not resist those two smiley faces. My daughter, two grandchildren, and I have been showing these wonderful little horses for over six years. I take photos at all of the shows and, of course, when the horses are born. I enjoy capturing candid shots of the kids; you can't imagine the expressions that appear on their faces when they are interacting with these beautiful animals.

PAROULEK, IVEL
This is a photo of a beautiful young woman, Linett A. Sierra. I met her in 2004 while representing the Parent Teacher Student Association of her high school. In 2004 Linett was going through the biggest challenge of her life. She came down with Hodgkin's lymphoma and went through chemotherapy and radiation. Linett missed seven months of her junior year and now, in May 2006 she will graduate in the top ten percent of her class. She has received a scholarship to a private college and wants to become a doctor. Linett will have a magical life now, and forever! "Eighteen And Alive" is a symbol of Linett's love for God, life, her family, and her friends!

PEACHEY, LORI
I'm a co-owner of a Curves franchise and I love taking pictures. During my pregnancy, all the ladies that attend Curves were there to support me. While on leave after the birth of my son, Nathan, my mom hung pictures of Nathan on the wall at Curves. Since then, I have had to keep hanging updated pictures. This one is of Nathan and his dog, Drag! The ladies loved it. They said I needed to enter it into a contest. One lady brought this contest in for me, so I sent it in. I can't wait to show her this book.

PELLICCIONE, NINA J.
This is a photo of our son, Mitchell. At the time this photo was taken he was three years old. We were spending the weekend at my parents' farm in Bindoon, Western Australia. Mitchell was wearing his grandfather's hat while having a picnic in the paddock with his brother, Nicholas, and sister, Kaylee. This picture shows the innocence that should be seen on all children's faces!

PENA, MARISELA
I shot this picture while filming a movie in the forest. When I saw him "thinking," I shot away to keep this image. That's why I like to keep the camera with me when I work, so I can keep those moments forever.

PERRIN, CHARLES J.
This is a photo of my wife, Marion. She is eighty-four years old, and the mother of twelve children and grandmother of twenty-two. She wanted to visit the monuments in Washington, D.C., and was thrilled that the cherry blossoms were rampant on the trees along the river. Marion is a naturally beautiful woman, and I have been privileged to be her husband for sixty-one years. I couldn't resist photographing her obvious joy among the beautiful blossoms. I think the title captures the moment in time when this photograph was taken.

PERRIN, MARLA MARIE
One of my favorite hobbies is taking pictures. I live in Washington State, so there are a lot of trails to walk through and many nature scenes all around. "Under The Pine Needles" was taken when my husband and I were on one of the trails. I wanted to take a picture that would be unique and different, I had no idea how the picture would turn out. At home downloading the pictures, I was shocked when I saw how it turned out. I hope you enjoy looking at my photo as much as I do.

PERRY, DONNA JEANNE
When our son and daughter-in-law came for a visit with our ten-week-old granddaughter, the adults decided to play a friendly game of euchre. We invited the baby to play a hand with us and with a little help from her mother, she did. However, she obviously thought she was playing a different game, as evidenced by her little poker face. I work for a local bank and my husband works for a local printer. Our immediate family consists of three exceptional sons, two energetic daughters-in-law, and one very special "Queen Of Hearts."

PERRY, NICOLE J.
This is a photo of my cats, Licker and Lucy, on Easter morning 2006. Licker thought the Easter basket was a new bed for him and he stayed in it all day! I love to take pictures and when I saw the two cats "posing" for me, I had to grab my camera and capture the moment.

PFEIFFER, CHELSEA
"Kolohe" means trouble in Hawaiian and "'Oli" means happy. So, my playful, little orange tabby's name is "Happy Trouble."

PIERSON, TAMMY MICHELLE
My family and I have always been somewhat fascinated with the paranormal. When we decided to take a trip to St. Augustine, Florida, we couldn't pass up the chance to experience some of the paranormal activities that take place within the city.

So, we set forth to check out some of the ghostly graveyards in St. Augustine, with our digital camera in hand. Upon our excursions to one of the city's creepiest graveyards, we captured this image on our digital camera. It looks like spooky white wisps of smoke. Although we're not sure what it is, we believe it is part of the many things in this world that are unexplainable!

PIRTLE, JAMES
I am a salvage diver. I travel all over the world and photography is a natural hobby for me. I took a day off and saw this little one with the chickens while I was walking around. I thought the picture came out well.

PLETSCHER, TREVA
You never know what a simple walk in the park may provide. This picture was taken while on a walk with my best friend and our five-year-old sons. This majestic hawk sat peacefully, watching us stroll by. What a pleasure it was!

POPE, RIKI
"After The Rain" is a continuation of my relationship with flowers and plants in my garden, or any other garden where I can get close to interesting subjects. I find nature photography a very rewarding endeavor.

PRANTE, WILLIAM ALLAN
This photo is of Mandy at Halloween. Normally, Mandy is very laid back, but gave this pose when she realized her candy was missing. She is a very loving, loyal friend of my wife, Sue, and I, and has been for the last ten years. I'm proud to share her photo and attitude with the world.

PRASINOS, GEORGE CONSTANTINOS
I was looking for photo opportunities, after a very bad rainstorm, in the morning. I found several and this was one of them. He was so soggy and wet he couldn't move, and it was just too good to pass up. He looked like he was mad at me for taking his picture before he could fix up his hair! He even grumbled about it. My father was a photographer in the Marines and I think I inherited his artistic eye. I've been photographing since the late 1960s. I look forward to taking more pictures.

RAINES, MARLA KATHLEEN
This is a photo of my daughter. I have always loved her eyes and her beautiful peach skin. I love taking photos but they mean even more to me when they are of her.

RAMBSEL, ALENE T.
This is a picture of my Chihuahua named Stephen. He was only nine months old when we took this picture. He loves to dress up and is very photogenic. I dedicate this picture to him because he has brought me so much joy and pleasure.

RANKIN, JANEL LYNN
This is a picture of perfectly designed pink roses, created by the hands of God. They are located in the state of Pennsylvania. The roses are planted in the front yard of our beautiful new home. My husband and I have two wonderful girls: Kali, four years old, and Madlyn, two. They love to help Mom pick the roses!

RAY, LAURA J.
My love of nature photography started in 1998 on a trip to Wyoming. The majestic mountain ranges started my love of landscape scenery. Over the years, my sense of knowing the perfect picture has become innate. My love for the mountains drives me to travel frequently in order to experience the happiness and serenity of nature, and her bounty.

RAYMOND, KIMBERLEE RENEE
I live in Riverton, Wyoming, with my husband, three children, and a chocolate Lab named Ruger. This photo was taken on July 4, 2005. While the children enjoyed the holiday festivities, we enjoyed the outdoors: camping, fishing, and gold prospecting. My husband and I both work outside the home, so we enjoy the time we spend on the weekends with our children. I enjoy taking pictures and this was just one of my many favorites of my son and his father.

REDRUP, MARGARET ANNE
This photo is of my husband, Garry, having a conversation with a Kea, a parrot of New Zealand. It looks like the Kea is saying, "Come on, where's the food." My husband was saying, "Can't you read the signs." We were on holiday in South Island, New Zealand, and as we came out of the Homer Tunnel, the Keas were in the car park. It was the first time I had seen them close up, so we stopped to take some photos. There were signs all around the car park warning not to feed these birds, but human nature takes over and a lot of people do just that. Keas are considered very intelligent, but also very cheeky.

REISTER, JOANNA L.
Anytime of the year in California, the topography of the Big Sur coastline is spectacular. Unlike any other area, the central coast from Carmel to San Simeon is truly a geological wonder. Springtime is a favorite season. The high tides encircle and blossoming wildflowers cling to the cliffs, artistically framing multitudes of hidden coves. Seeking them out is well worth it. I came upon this striking outlook through a magnificent glen of cypress and redwood trees. Here is my photograph, "The Hidden Cove — Big Sur Coastline, California."

ROBERTS, HANNAH MARIE
I became interested in photography shortly before I took this photograph, my sophomore year at Wasburn Rural High School in Kansas. I love taking pictures of my brother and four sisters. This is my favorite picture of my sister, Amariah, because it captures her quiet, introverted, and innocent nature.

RODRIGUEZ, SABELLA MONIN
This picture was taken in March 2006. My grandmother, Mary Sabella, is holding my daughter, Olivia Midori Hotaling. Olivia is five months old in this picture and Mary is eighty-three. Olivia is Mary's first great-grandchild. This was Olivia's first trip to Manhattan from Florida to see her "Gi Gi." Mary lives on the twelfth floor and you can see Manhattan in the background. Although it was very cold, Olivia had a wonderful time meeting her family.

RODRIGUEZ, SUSAN
This photo was taken on our family vacation to my husband's hometown, Guayama, Puerto Rico. My son, Joel, saw these two mannequins (the bottom halves only) and proceeded to pose with his arms around their "waists." I saw the opportunity to capture a great candid moment on film.

ROGERS, KRISTI LYNN
While visiting the Piankatank River in Gloucester, Virginia, one weekend, I noticed an osprey searching the river for fish. His mate was sitting on the nest, and he would find food and take it to her. I was able to capture him on film in mid-flight. This magnificent creature returns to this beautiful location every year. Here he knows the fish are plentiful and his offspring will prosper. With his wings spread, it is almost as though he knew his picture was being taken. I plan to keep watching with the hope of getting a glimpse of his offspring as they make their first flight!

ROSE, NICHOLAS MATTHEW
I've always loved aviation and photography, ever since I was a young child. I was a photographer in my high school yearbook class. I enjoying taking pictures at the San Francisco International Airport. One morning, I went to the airport; it was a wonderful, sunny day with lots of aviation traffic. While panning for a shot, I noticed one of the local birds standing on a light. I could see, in the background, a line of aircraft waiting to take off, and a couple landing. So, I decided to take a picture that shows two different types of flight. It makes me think about the past when early mankind looked at the bird and wondered, "How can we take to the skies like the birds?"

ROSENBERG, FRED
This photo was taken on Independence Day in Bridgehampton, New York. The morning was perfect: warm, sunny, ready for the myriad of parades, barbecues, and family outings. While flags were everywhere — on public buildings, lawns, and draped from homes — none of them showed the colors, nor welcomed the day ahead more dramatically than the Stars and Stripes in this photo.

RUPPA, MARLENE ROSE
My late husband, Robert, played Santa every year he was physically able to do so. His love of children and life showed on his beautiful face every day of his life. It was his smile that attracted me to him, and eventually I became his wife. "Santa's Sweet Smiles" will remain etched in my mind and heart forever, until we meet again.

RUSSELL, KAREN E.
This is our three-year-old daughter, Kara Skye, in the car, going home after a hospital appointment. Kara is our only child and she is so precious to us. I took this photo because it captures the life of a three-year-old after a long day, she is too tired to even take her bottle out of her mouth. My husband, Allan, and I are so lucky to have such a beautiful little girl who is the apple of our eye. Allan is a baker and I work for Australian Post, and the best thing about coming home at night from work is the huge welcome Kara gives me as I walk in the front door.

RUSSO, ALLISON
This photo was taken on my first trip to New York City. I love how the buildings are reflected in the nighttime skyline. New York City can be overwhelming because of its size, but it looks so peaceful from this view. I love New York.

RUSSO, ANNA M.
At six in the morning, the village was bustling with activity. The animals were heading out to pasture and the men to their cornfields. Meanwhile, the women were fetching water from the well. Amidst all of this, Asta and her three grandsons were having breakfast; a simple meal of porridge that tasted a little tart and slightly sweet, yet was the perfect beginning to a long day. After living for two years in this tiny African village, I will never forget the simplicity of life, the friendships I developed, or waking up to perfect moments like this one.

RUTH, JENNIFER D.
This is a picture of my daughter and stepdaughter. They love getting dressed up and taking glamour shots. They both love the fact that the pictures make them look so much older than they really are. They are only eleven years old, by the way. Not such great news for us parents, huh? But, they are very beautiful and they take great pictures!

RYAN, JOHN RICHARD
As the sun starts to set in the winter, the sky turns a foreboding purple and night approaches. My "girls" arrive, along with the rest of the family and a few visiting neighbors. It's time to feast, with whole corn and grains, topped with a mixture of molasses. I enjoy caring for the deer that are looking for a bit of help during the winter; it is my treat in life!

SABARESE, ROSALIE
I was born and raised in upstate New York and currently reside in Florida. I am an artist of many different types of media: jewelry design, photography, abstract painting, and sculpture. With the encouragement and love from each member of my family and friends, I've been able to express myself through art. This photo, "Little Girl Lost," tells a story we all share, one of hidden fears with hopeful eyes.

SALAY, JAMES PAUL
As a sculptor and freelance photographer, I sincerely believe the essence of photography is composition, light, exposure, and timing. The goal is to capture a unique moment of composition in time, a picture that tells a story. This photo was taken on the Gold Coast of Florida and shows a tanker vessel offshore, pointing in the same direction as the man's body in the sand. Visually, the man's body becomes a vessel, the palm trunk the mast of a sail, and the fronds of the palm become the sail. I imagine both vessels embarking on an endless journey.

SALO, THERESA MARIE
I love any form of art, and when I came upon the medium of photography, I was in heaven. I am now attending school for photo imaging in Staples, Minnesota, and have never been happier.

SANSBURY, TAYLER HUMES
This photograph is one of many self-portraits. I get into these moods of taking pictures and I like to have interesting backgrounds, or other objects that really stand out to me. In this picture, the sign is a wall decoration that I placed on the floor beside me. This one was actually taken with a camera phone, and I was really surprised how well it turned out. My family likes to send pictures back and forth to each other and I really enjoy sharing my work with family and friends.

SARKAR, JOLLY
This is a photograph that I took when I got my digital camera. I still remember the moment directly after the strong thunderstorm that passed through. My husband, Arun, and our son, Ankit, were outside playing while I was in the garden. It was just beautiful to see the flowers and the butterflies in the garden after a fresh rain. I just couldn't stop myself and grabbed my camera to capture the moment.

SCHMIDT, KARI LEE
This photo was taken in New York City. It's a very large water fountain. I don't believe in changing any aspects of my photos, what I see is what you get. I own an art gallery in Chillicothe, Illinois; it is a dream come true. I owe everything to our Heavenly Father above! Enjoy and God bless.

SCHNAITMAN, KELSEY
This picture was taken around Christmas while my friends were home from school. I often have small get-togethers, so we can catch up and have a good time. This image is of my friend, Colleen, and my wineglass. I take images of objects and try to personify them. The wineglass appears to be the focal point; it is almost like the glass is imagining itself being used by someone else. Taking photographs is what I love to do, and one day I would like a photography studio of my own.

SCHULTZ, KAREN LYNDOE
Like most things in my life, I chose a hobby I can't financially afford, the expensive art form of photography. Thanks to my parents, three older brothers, their families, and my wonderful boyfriend, Jimi, for giving me the things I need to pursue my love of photography. Generally, the subjects I capture are quite abstract. I live in Annapolis, Maryland, with Jimi and our two boxers: Norton and Mayble. They continually provide the community and myself with the silliest photo opportunities. They are known to make even the grumpy smile.

SELTZER, MICHELLE DAWN
In the last three months, I've discovered photography! Since then, I've taken approximately five thousand pictures! I watch so many passers-by that seem oblivious to the most amazing facets of this world. I want to scream, "Look at those colors, those reflections, those textures, those expressions!" Now, I've uncovered an ideal way to share the world I see with others. This is a photo of one of my favorite subjects, my children. These sweet models provide me with moments everywhere I turn. In regards to this picture, not to worry, the photographed tracks are virtually abandoned!

SHANMUGASUNDARAM, RAMESH
This is a photo of my daughter, Miranyaa, age two-and-a-half. This is my first trip to the United States with my family. I am a math teacher from India, now working in High Point, North Carolina. My hobby is photography. I love to take pictures and share them with friends and relatives. I am here in the country as a cultural ambassador. My goal is to give values and culture to this country's young citizens.

SHARBER, GLORIA
This is a photo taken during my trip to Maui in September 2004. My husband and I were leaving Kaanapali Beach because it was raining when, all of a sudden, this wonderful rainbow appeared. It caught my attention and I knew I had to capture this magical moment.

SHENKER, INNA
Life is full of moments to live by. This photo was taken on February 12, 2006 during a snowstorm in Brooklyn, New York. On that day, the owner stepped outside and did not seem too happy due to the lack of customers. After he went in, I took the picture of the grocery store and the train to show how empty it was. I enjoy the winter, along with all the other seasons. However, the winter brings snow. I feel that snow makes a picture look historic, even if it is taken in the twenty-first century.

SHEWBRIDGE, LORIE JEAN
After a day of gift opening and a delicious meal, my husband, his son, and his son's dog decided to relax in front of the television. It was not long after I took this picture that all three were snoring, very satisfied and happy! It made me feel so lucky to be surrounded by my family, and everyone was happy and healthy.

SIMMONS, FREDERICK
I am a police officer in Detroit, Michigan. One night while working on patrol, I was dispatched to a homicide scene. This photograph reminded me of that moment. Although the photo was taken during a play, I couldn't help but shake this eerie feeling that I experienced. It is truly strange how art often imitates life.

SINGH, ZAHIN
"The Calm" has a very deep meaning. I created it to remind us that the destructive forces of nature cannot destroy the beauty we find everywhere. The picture was taken the day after Hurricane Rita destroyed Cozumel, Mexico, in 2005. The hurricane caused over ten million dollars in damage. The world's most destructive forces continuously destroy the most fragile areas. I am a photographer who uses my pictures as a journal for my travels, experiences, knowledge, and wisdom. They say a picture tells a thousand words, but I believe it also tells what words cannot.

SISTO, ROSEMARY
I like taking photos of nature. While driving down Route 30 in West Dummerston, Vermont, I saw ice hanging down from ledges with fresh snow below. I thought it would make a wonderful photograph. I am a grandmother of nine and soon to be a great-grandmother. I guess there's always

a photo to take. My husband and I paint houses every day, and during the summer I do a few craft shows. Thank you for selecting my photograph, it's an honor!

SKIDMORE, CYNDI ANN
Michigan's Upper Peninsula, with its magical balance between land and water, provided an opportunity to capture the beauty of an overcast summer day. Lake Michigan appears to become one with the sky in the creation of an endless horizon. Only nature can offer this flawless simplicity, and only a higher being can combine all of the elements. A nature photographer is an observer and a recorder. The camera shutter merely freezes the scene to share a brief moment in the gift of creation.

SKILES, KIMBERLY ANNE
Photography is my passion and my favorite subject is my daughter, Alexis. This picture was taken on Easter. It was one of those special moments that are such a delight to capture. As we all know, children are the essence of innocence.

SMITH, ANN MARIE
On a warm December day, our granddaughter, Kimberly, then age two, came to visit. Since her family lived in the country outside of town (where West Texas winds blow away everything not fastened down), she had never seen so many leaves in one place. Playing together under our huge pecan tree, we marched through the piles, jumped in them, and then I had her mother throw them in the air to fall like pennies from Heaven. God himself controlled the timing of the shutter on my camera and the result, "Autumn Wonder," is now a family treasure.

SMITH, KATHRYN ELIZABETH GRACE
Meet Miss Molly. Having a bad hair day is a common occurrence, but today for this photo her look said it all. For my husband, James, and I, she has shone a light and brought so much happiness, laughter, and love. She knows what we are thinking when we are with her. Having our two children grown up, married, and having their own children (we have four grandchildren now), we needed something in our home to love. Molly has six pet cats and one cockatoo to play with. She represents nearly fifty percent of my photo taking these days.

SMITH, RONALD J.
This is a picture of our good friend, Charlie, along with our three raccoons he helped my fiancée, Val, and I raise. Their mother was killed shortly after they were born. We had to take turns bottle-feeding them every few hours. Charlie retired in 1983 so he could care for them while Val and I worked. Bear, Runt, and Chubby adopted us all as their parents and were by our sides every day. Once grown, we slowly introduced them back into the wild; well sort of, they now live in the rafters of Charlie's barn.

SNIPP, RON LEE
The tranquility that each picture represents to its individual viewer, and the beauty of nature, have inspired my photography.

SNYDER, HAYLEE
This is a photograph of a sunset that I took outside of my house. I was taking pictures one day because it is something I love to do. I saw how beautiful the sunset looked and decided to photograph it. I think the colors in the sky add so much to this picture.

SNYDER, CLARENCE JOHN, JR.
Of the many flowers in our garden, we like day lilies the most. "Star Rising" captures one of the most beautiful flowers I have ever seen. The many colors and styles of flowers give us much enjoyment. Thank you for letting us show you just one of many.

SPARCELLO, RANDY CHRISTOPHER
Butch was my son and best friend for nine short years. The day I found out he had cancer, and only two months to live, my heart crumbled into pieces. After two rolls of film, this is the only picture that developed due to my camera malfunctioning. I found this out after it was too late. My son is now gone, but I have this astonishing photo to remember him by. I see the love in my boy's eyes and that's why I titled this photograph, "Love, In Memory Of Butch (March 1997–December 2005)."

SPENCER, DEBRA ANN
Matthew was five years old in this picture. He is shown holding a salmon while on a fishing trip in Alaska. His expression truly reflects his love and joy of fishing. Matthew named this photograph. He is now seven years old.

SPROLES, BRYAN DAVIDSON
This photo was taken during a European trip in 2004. We stopped in Oswiecim, Poland, to visit the concentration camp. While at Auschwitz-Birkenau, I saw this small Israeli flag lying in the rubble at the back of the camp and knew immediately that I had to take this photo.

ST. JACQUES, RAYMOND
I had the pleasure of visiting Italy during the summer of 1998. In rushing through the very crowded streets of beautiful, romantic Venice, I came upon these four lovely ladies standing outside a little dress shop. Somehow, I managed to persuade the mass of people to stop for a few seconds, enabling me to take this shot. One of these beauties seemed to be saying, "That's our style."

STATON, TOM
It was a chilly afternoon at a beach in Rhode Island. I was standing out on some rocks, snapping shots of the beach, when I looked up and took this picture. When you look at this photo, imagine the sounds of the waves and the smell of the water. The spot was very relaxing, but cold. I think I took this around November. I hope everyone that sees this likes it.

STAVRAKIS, VASILIKI ANGELINE
The story behind "Falling In Love In Greece," is the story of unrequited love that occurred on an enchanted evening. Two hearts and souls became one, not in the physical sense, but rather the metaphysical sense. As I lay on the Aegean seashore, I made a wish, "I love you, I miss you, I wish you were here." What manifested was not the three-quarter-shaped moon apparent in the dark, cloud-less evening, but rather a heart-shaped moon. I believe it was an expression of our hearts and souls becoming one.

STEWART, NATALIE L.
I took this photo at the Makgadikgadi Pans National Park in Botswana, earlier this year while in Africa. I am originally from Zimbabwe, but now live in London, England, due to the terrible economic state in my native country. I go back to Africa once a year and try to see as much as I can. I love taking photos in the African bush: the animals, the sunsets, and the sunrises. Africa is a continent untouched in so many ways. The innocence and the beauty are things everyone should experience. If only we could take all of the sadness away somehow.

STREETER, MICHAEL THOMAS
This is a photo of a newly painted lift bridge on Lake Ontario. It was taken in early spring 2006 at about seven in the morning, just after sunrise. Despite the warm look of the photo, it was actually pretty cold outside.

STROMAN, AARON
This photo is a result of too much free time in a coffee shop.

STUCK, COURTNEY
This is a photo of my younger sister, Bonnie. It was taken on a bridge at our grandparent's house out in the country. I wanted to show that even the most familiar of places could also look strange, even dangerous. The rubber boots belong to my grandma. I'm currently attending Southern Illinois University at Carbondale, and photography is just one of my many hobbies.

SULLIVAN, CRYSTAL LYNN
This is a photo of my three-year-old Maltese, Prince Sullivan of Mallory Valley, otherwise known as "Sully." "Sully" loves to have his picture taken and he gets jealous when I take pictures of people, or other dogs. He is playing the piano in this picture.

SWARTZ, ALISON LEIGH
This is a portrait of my friend, John Lodge. He is a very outgoing person and this shows his more quiet side. I am currently a photographer and graphic designer for a local newspaper. I'm always looking for new opportunities.

TEGYI, RACHEL L.
Dear Mya, I hope you will own this book and maybe, pass it on to your children many, many years to come. We love you greatly. Love always, Mom and Dad. This is a picture of my daughter, Mya Lyn Sebring, at seven months old, posing on her daddy's motorcycle.

THOMAS, MELISSA TITUS
I was expecting my son, Jackson, when Hurricane Katrina devastated New Orleans. He was born a day before Thanksgiving and we could not be more thankful. He was a light in our lives in a time of difficulty. This picture was taken before his baptism on March 19, 2006. Jackson was smiling at his grandfather, John, and turned to look at the camera. He truly is a joy.

TIMKO-HOCHKEPPEL, KENDRA A.
I enjoy taking pictures from time to time. When I had my daughter, Carisa, I started to take lots of pictures of her! In this photo, Carisa was only three-and-a-half months old. When it was her last feeding before her bedtime, she would just fall asleep while she was drinking at the same time. I love the way she looks when she does that. I had to take a picture of her so she can see what she was like as a baby! It is an honor that my photo was selected for publication! Thank you!

TROUBLEFIELD, MARY SUSAN
I have always loved taking pictures! I'm the family member no one sees in photos because I'm always the one taking them. This is a picture of my son playing with a blanket. I have two children and am always trying to get them to pose for me. I truly believe that as our memories fade, pictures will tell our stories!

TRUDEAU, SUE MARIE
Lily is our six-week-old daughter who is usually always smiling. This look was made after her sister, Rosie, made a loud screeching sound. What a grumpy look!

TURNER, JEN
This picture came from the first roll of film that I took with my new SLR. I didn't expect much. Somehow, I managed to capture a wonderful photo of my girls. It is one of my favorite.

TURNER, THOMAS MARTIN
This is a photograph of the remaining members of the 69th New York State Volunteer Infantry, one of the regiments of the Irish Brigade from the Civil War. I normally don't take the shots because I am in the thick of the fighting! However, in this case, I got caught short of ammo and had to take a "hit." I went down in a good spot to snap a few shots off with the camera, instead of the rifle.

TUTTLE, GERALD LEE
This photo was taken using a Nikon camera. There has not been any photo adjustments or special effects done after the photo was taken. At the time I made this photo, the model, Joy, and myself had very little hands-on experience in the field. I had a vision that I was able to produce with little planning and set up, using a large mirror with properly placed lighting and camera angles. With this combination, I brought out the artistic beauty of the model's face, eyes, and body shape.

TYLER, MELISSA
This is a picture of my sister's son, Jacob. I love this picture, not only because of the beautiful tulips, but because if I get just one peek into his eyes, I can see all the love this little man has. It makes me hope for the day that I have a son just like him. I love you, Jacob!

ULRICH, JESSICA JO
This photo was taken at the college rodeo held at Eastern Oregon University during the fall 2005. It is of a great friend of mine, Sonny Hansen. Sonny is the rodeo coach at Treasure Valley Community College and is a pickup man for many rodeos in the Northwest. I have loved photography and rodeo all my life. I am extremely excited that I am able to share this photo with others.

UNDERWOOD, LINDA
This is a photo of my ten-year-old daughter, Julie, waiting for her age division to dance in Conway, Arkansas. The temperature was over one hundred degrees Fahrenheit. Julie is a jingle dancer and has been dancing since she was three years old. I love to take pictures of my children and grandchildren. I almost forgot to tell you, Julie won first place!

VALENTIN, JERRY
"Lighthouse Cabo Rojo" was taken two hundred feet from a cliff; I was riding in a Black Hawk Helicopter. The picture was taken around eleven in the morning with a Canon digital. I am a helicopter technician and I like to take my cameras when I go flying with the crew. Puerto Rico is beautiful. I am very pleased to know that the world will be able to see just how beautiful this island is because of my picture. This photo is dedicated to my wife, Maritza Mendez.

VANDYKE, DAVID ARTHUR
My wife and I were attending the Goodguys Custom Car Show in Pleasanton, California. I was taking pictures of the cars when I noticed this fellow. In particular, I observed the similarities between him and the car, especially his low pants. Looking at the picture later on the computer, I saw several more similarities. Taking photos is a fun hobby.

VANG, MAI SAO
As a child, I've always played with my dad's camera. I never knew that photography and travel were my passions. I believe that traveling broadens one's view, you can focus on what you're looking for. I came from a big family of picture-takers. We like to collect and reminisce about pictures from past to present. This is a photo of my niece, Paige, at four months. She'll grow older, but this picture never will.

VAROUHAKIS, ANGELA
This is a photo that I took of my boyfriend, Michael. He is from New Jersey, United States of America. Coming from the Northern Hemisphere, his first time on a picture-perfect, sun-drenched Australian beach was a priceless moment. I couldn't keep him out of the water; he was like a child on Christmas morning. When I captured this moment on film he was unaware of my presence. After hours in the surf, the look of contentment on his face says it all.

VELAZQUEZ, ELIAN
This picture was taken when I was sailing down to Fajardo, a small town on the East Coast of Puerto Rico. I took this picture so that people could really appreciate the beauty of a sunset; something that people can't do because of the fast-pace society we live in.

VIRAMONTES, LINDA
I took this photo on the way home from visiting my dad in Nevada. We had just driven through a storm and it was clearing away. My kids, knowing that I love clouds, saw this in the distance. My daughter said, "Mom, it looks like Heaven." So, I snapped this shot through the closed window while my husband was driving. When I got home, I downloaded my picture and saw that there were three electrical poles in the distance and they looked liked crosses in the light.

VIVIRITO, JULIE
My husband and I went on vacation to New Orleans, Louisiana, in April 2005. It was a beautiful spring day in Jackson Square and many artists were there, painting and displaying their work. We had a fantastic time visiting "The Big Easy." The friendly people, delicious food, and great music made it one of the best trips we've ever taken. Our thoughts and prayers go out to the victims of Hurricane Katrina. I am a registered nurse and I live with my wonderful husband, and our three cats, in Wisconsin.

VO, HUONG
Anytime I travel, I always have a camera with me. I love taking pictures because it's something sentimental for me to hold onto. Catching moments is something I will always cherish because I know the moment I take the picture, it can never occur again. It's the "simple things" in life that make me smile, so this rose at the Public Market Center in Seattle, Washington, was what made my day. I had to hold onto that and share it with others.

WALLACE, POLLY
I took this picture of a mushroom in Silverton, Colorado. I was on a hike and spotted the lovely mushroom on a dead limb. Photographer Polly Wallace brings the spirit and passion to landscape photography. She thoroughly enjoys experiencing the great outdoors. Polly considers Colorado a treasure to be shared with those that appreciate natural scenic beauty. Polly was born in Montrose, Colorado. She is deaf and uses sign language to communicate. She graduated from the National Technology Institute for the Deaf in Rochester, New York. She lives in Montrose and loves to take photographs of natural scenic beauty. She is an avid outdoor woman, she captures the creative wisdom of nature as an art form to uplift and inspire the human spirit.

WALSH, BRITTANY RAY
My daughter, Brittany, perceives the world in an interesting, unique way. Her personality and charm allow her to reveal objects that would normally be disguised, or camouflaged. Her passion, creativity, and zealous style give her the ability to make you see what she wants you to. She brilliantly incorporates herself into all of her work. Anyone can accidentally take a wonderful photograph. Only a gifted artist can make you feel, or see something special. We are so proud of you! Because of you, this world is a better place.

WALSH, SHAWN MICHAEL
This picture is of a railroad bridge outside Yuma, Arizona. Lately, I have been driving a lot and I get bored looking at the road, so my eyes start wondering. When I saw this, I knew I had to take a picture and share it with others. With this place being out of the way, they wouldn't have been able to experience this awesome landscape.

WATSON, GRANT RICHARD
While backpacking around Australia during a gap year in 2004 I managed to capture this photo during a thunderstorm in Sydney. After hanging out of my apartment window for almost an hour, I eventually captured this bolt of lightening striking somewhere in the city. I took almost one hundred photos and have only this one to show for my efforts. It was worth the wait.

WAYNE, MICHELLE EMILY
My interest in photography started in middle school. My parents bought me a great camera a few years after that. I have had fun taking pictures with it. "Smelling The Flower" is of my nephew, Clayton, when he was two years old. I asked him to smell the flower. I don't know why he put it to his forehead, but it adds to the charm of the picture.

WEAVER, AMANDA
Little Marisa is the most curious child I've ever known! When she came upon this huge truck her daddy built, we sat back and watched her marvel at the enormity of the tire alone! She was able to see her reflection in the chrome rim of the wheel and got quite excited at the little girl "looking" back at her! Nothing seems to scare my little baby, but I guess that's why I'm here, to do the worrying for her.

WEIGHT, JESSICA
This photo is of my dog, Rain. We were playing in the snow with her tennis ball and I kept trying to get good pictures of her. I captured two that have become my favorites so far. This is one of those two. I'm currently attending Salt Lake Community College to earn my associate's degree in photography.

WEISMAN, ALEC B.
After growing up around photography, my interests appeared when I got my first digital camera. Fostered by three years of working as a student volunteer guide at the Los Angeles Zoo, my photography has improved tremendously. This stunning photograph was captured at Westlake Village, California, and this was the only time I have ever seen swans there.

WENNICK, DIANNE
This is a photo of my niece, Maria, with her friends, Mattie and Marie. My sister, Sharisse, prepared a special spa day for the girls. They had facials and later, went to the steam room. Their idea of taking a steam wasn't to sit and relax. Instead, they made funny faces on the glass! I took a photo when I realized that this was a special moment. When I first saw the photo, I wasn't quite sure what it was. Somehow, the photo took on a life of its own and definitely captured the essence of children at play.

WESTALL, EDWARD J.
Throughout my lifetime, I have taken thousands of photographs. I have observed that the most memorable ones are the spontaneous pictures, like this one of my granddaughter, Rhiannon, who has cerebral palsy. I captured this image as she sat in her wheelchair, happy and content, silhouetted by the light of the window. I quickly grabbed my camera and snapped the picture, capturing a precious little moment in time. Isn't that what photography is all about?

WESTBERRY, PAULA IRENE
I took this photo while cruising on the restored section of the Kissimmee River in Central Florida. This proud tree stood alone on the riverbank, reminding me of ages past. Unfortunately, this picture is the only image that remains; Hurricane Charlie toppled the tree in 2004. As a child, I witnessed my grandfather's passion for nature photography and have placed this photo next to his award-winning photo of a New England oak; the circle is completed.

WHEREAT, ADRIAN
I have been taking photographs since the age of sixteen. However, since 1986 technology has excelled and so has my interest in photography, and my ability to create beautiful pictures. "Sunset Stone Throw" was captured while we were taking a leisurely stroll along the beach at Weston Super Mare, England. Our son, Harry, was throwing stones in the sea, with a stunning sky as a backdrop. I couldn't resist capturing this moment.

WHITE, REBECCA A.
Simplicity is one of the most overlooked forms of beauty.

WICK, MELISSA JO
When I captured the picture of this little girl, she was walking with her father. She represents his hope and, for me, she symbolized the next generation and our hope for the future. My photo captures that curiosity, that innocence that we often try to regain, or relive as adults. I love photography for its ability to document the true essence of a person and relay a feeling that we can experience again, if only for a second.

WILSON, KAREN I.
Photography began as a hobby for me. I quickly learned, however, that photographs can capture the soul and it is now becoming a passion. This picture was taken the day after Hurricane Ivan hit the island of Granada. This young girl lived in this small house with her mother and brother, just in front of my grandmother's home. Before I took the picture, she was drying her clothes. It reminded me of the devastation that natural disasters can cause, and the incredible resilience of the human spirit.

WIMBERLY, LISA KAY
I took this picture on the actual Gilligan's Island, located in the Bahamas, in June 2004. My daughters, Ashley and Andrea, ages twenty and sixteen, and I travel internationally every summer. While standing there, I felt like I was trapped in time with the view, thus the title of my photo was born. Ashley, whom is in college, is the real photographer in our family since her photos look like postcards. I believe life is a continuous journey of learning and change. If you are lucky enough to find yourself in a beautiful place, you can forget everything for a short time.

WISHART, AMANDA KARLY
My "mama's boy" cat, Junior, is known for squeezing himself into small, weird places and going to sleep. In addition to this shoebox storage container, he likes dust pans, plant pots, and wire baskets. My little troublemaker looks so innocent when he sleeps.

WOLFE, JESSIE
I have a passion for photography. I have always been in love with the moments, the colors, and the nostalgia that a great picture can capture. I am so fortunate to be surrounded by people that give me constant inspiration. This particular photo is of my two-year-old daughter, Jayda. She was caught off guard when I busted her with birthday cake all over her face that morning. She looked as if she wanted to say, "Who, me?" It is such an honor to be published; I am so excited and proud. Thank you for this vote of confidence as I pursue my career with photography.

WONG, HOI SHAN
I love children; they are the most beautiful images in my world. I love to watch them play and take pictures of them. It reminds me of my happy childhood with my mother, sister, and brother, and the best moment I have captured on film will live forever as "Fun At The Beach." I am an amateur photographer. I enjoy taking photographs at home, or while on holiday. I enjoy being creative and artistic. Taking photographs allows me to create images in a way that shows how I see the word.

WONG, MAGGIE
This is a photo of our first baby, Marissa, at six months old. She was born five weeks early, but has grown wonderfully, learning everything quickly. Here, she has just discovered the use of her tongue. My husband, Eddie, and I can't believe how time flies and how quickly she has grown. She gives us expressions that just melt our hearts away on a daily basis. We keep a camera nearby at all times just to catch these special moments, forever in time.

WONG, MELVIN
I was traveling through China when I became awestruck by the beauty of the waterways in the city of Suzhou. I took this photograph because of Marco Polo; he once traveled to this city on its waterway. The thought inspired me to take this beautiful picture.

WOODWORTH, DEVIN
I love to take pictures of people and beautiful scenery — moments in my life I want to remember. It's impossible to retain all the wonderful memories inside your head, but with pictures you can refresh your memory anytime you want. That is why I always keep my camera with me, so I can capture the memories if I want to. But, one of the best things about capturing my memories on film is that I can share them with other people.

WRIGHT, KAITLYN
This photo is of my son and husband — I love taking pictures of them. Logan is our first child. This is the first time I was able to capture Logan on film with a hat on; he usually throws them off before I can snap the photo. I've taken many pictures of Logan throughout the fifteen months he's been with us, but this one showed how happy he really is. It also shows how he wants to be just like his

daddy. I love how he's holding Daddy's hand in the photo. Logan truly is my "sweet baby boy."

WRIGHT, PHYLLIS MAE

I often don't take pictures because they don't come out right, but this one was different. I thought this photograph was so cute! This picture is of my five-year-old son, Cody A. Wright, playing around. I took this photo and submitted it because it captured his innocence and at the same time, how cute he is. I wanted to preserve his face and the moment forever.

WRIGHT, RACHAEL LEIGH

My family is amazing. We have always been really close and this is mostly thanks to Mimi, Tiny Bray, and my granddaddy, Sam Bracy III. They brought us all together for a fun family vacation in Florida. We always look forward to our yearly trip. Mimi passed away in December 2004 but our tradition continues. Even though she will not be there in body, she will always be there in spirit. We will continue with our lives and the endless possibilities life has to offer. The love we have for each other makes this possible.

WRINN, FRANK W., JR.

When you capture a moment of happiness — a boy's dream — it's something you will never forget. Dalton is seven years old now and enjoys bikes, cars, and sports. Berry and Amy, Dalton's parents, spend lots of time taking him to and from his activities. I am proud to be his grandfather and share time in my little buddy's life. I believe that if he grips the handlebars of life tight enough, he will become the true "American boy." Photos like this will always tell a story.

ZERA, BEATA

This is a photo of myself. All people on Earth are unique — no two are the same. I love taking pictures in order to capture things that might be missed when looking at objects the first time. I have dedicated this picture to my husband and my son; both help me every day. They are a never-ending source of support for me while I attend school to earn my bachelor's degree in criminal justice. I also dedicate this picture to my sister, my younger siblings, and my parents. Thank you.

ZIELINSKI, MORGAN BROOKE

This is a picture of my two dogs: Paladin and Mackenzie. Paladin, seven months old, is a Siberian husky, born in Illinois. He loves playing in the snow, catching birds, and swimming. Mackenzie, six months old, is a yellow Lab, born in Minnesota. She is full of energy, and loves swimming and taking up half the bed at night. Paladin and Mackenzie are affectionate dogs who love everyone they come into contact with.

ZIRPOLI, ROBERT JOHN

My wife, Karen, and I spent a weekend on our boat in the Potomac River, anchoring in different coves in Virginia and Maryland. I awoke around five in the morning with intentions of taking pictures of the sunrise. As the sun started rising, fishermen were netting from left to right. Using my Canon EOS-20D I waited, hoping the fishermen would cross the reflection of the sunrise. Before the sun got too high and lost its glow, I took this photo. I've been photographing the beauty of life for over forty years.

ZSIDO, ALETHA LEANN

Trekking through the Western Himalayas of Nepal led me onto the Tibetan Plateau. Here, I found myself on a pilgrimage to the ancient, sacred land of Muktinath. As I wandered outside the main temple walls, a weathered woman waved to me from within a small building. She motioned that I sit across from her as she began chanting in a low drone. We spun the enlarged, colorfully chipped and cracked prayer wheel together. Then, she let me take her picture. My photography captures the spirit of my travels by portraying the natural beauty of people and unique perspectives on the environment.

INDEX OF
PHOTOGRAPHERS